The New York Times

IN THE HEADLINES

Drug Kingpins

THE PEOPLE BEHIND DRUG TRAFFICKING

THE NEW YORK TIMES EDITORIAL STAFF

Published in 2021 by New York Times Educational Publishing in association with The Rosen Publishing Group, Inc.
29 East 21st Street, New York, NY 10010

First Edition

The New York Times
Caroline Que: Editorial Director, Book Development
Phyllis Collazo: Photo Rights/Permissions Editor
Heidi Giovine: Administrative Manager

Rosen Publishing
Megan Kellerman: Managing Editor
Alexander Pappas: Editor
Greg Tucker: Creative Director
Brian Garvey: Art Director   APR 1 9 2021

Cataloging-in-Publication Data
Names: New York Times Company.
Title: Drug kingpins: the people behind drug trafficking / edited by the New York Times editorial staff.
Description: New York : New York Times Educational Publishing, 2021. | Series: In the headlines | Includes glossary and index.
Identifiers: ISBN 9781642823394 (library bound) | ISBN 9781642823387 (pbk.) | ISBN 9781642823400 (ebook)
Subjects: LCSH: Drug traffic—Juvenile literature. | Drug dealers—Juvenile literature. | Drug control—Juvenile literature.
Classification: LCC HV5809.5 D784 2021 | DDC 363.45—dc23

Manufactured in the United States of America

On the cover: Drug kingpin Joaquín "El Chapo" Guzmán is escorted to a helicopter by security forces at Mexico City International Airport, Feb. 22, 2014; Susana Gonzalez/ Bloomberg/Getty Images.

Contents

CHAPTER 2

Latin America and the Drug Trade

CHAPTER 3

The Rule of Pablo Escobar

Introduction

NARCOTICS HAVE A LONG and complicated history. They have at times been deemed lawful, and at other times, considered illicit contraband. Some former illegal opiates, for instance, are now employed for medical purposes; however, not all narcotics have beneficial qualities. Indeed, some take a devastating toll. In the modern era, drugs such as heroin, cocaine, ecstasy and methamphetamine conjure the darkest images of violence and addiction.

These sinister connotations are well-earned. In Mexico, drug cartels and the kingpins who lead them play such a prevalent role that they directly impact every level of local and national government. While in the United States our perspective can be myopic, other countries continue to struggle against the current of the global drug trade. In the Philippines, President Rodrigo Duterte has launched a ruthless, extra-judicial military campaign to oust powerful drug cartels. In Colombia, the unofficial capital and chief exporter of cocaine, drug cartels held the country at ransom politically and economically for most of the late 20th century. In Afghanistan, American troops and national guards have been unable to contain the popular resurgence of an old face: opium.

The leaders of these narcotrafficking businesses are commonly known as drug kingpins. While they deal primarily in narcotics, drug kingpins' résumés commonly include terrorism, human trafficking, political assassinations and fomenting violent civil unrest.

Some have had even more unique abilities that have allowed them to expand their power: Frank Lucas was able to exploit the political upheaval of the Vietnam War to his advantage. By negotiating with corrupt U.S. military officials based in Vietnam and Thailand,

Joaquín Archivaldo Guzmán Loera, more famously known as El Chapo, at La Palma prison in Almoloya de Juárez, Mexico, in July 1993.

Lucas was able to smuggle narcotics directly from the Golden Triangle into Harlem, using the coffins of deceased servicemen to avoid detection. Paul Le Roux was able to fully utilize digital technology to remain anonymous and expand his control over global heroin trafficking. Le Roux initially funded his empire by identifying the niche market of low-cost prescription pharmaceuticals in the United States and fostering a legitimate business. Others, like El Chapo, were able to play upon local loyalties of corrupt government officials and preexisting animosities to consolidate his power. Through his charisma and network, El Chapo nearly monopolized all drug trafficking across the Mexican border with the United States.

No other drug kingpin has yet to surpass the legacy of Pablo Escobar. At times magnetic, egotistical and audacious, Escobar exploited the political turmoil that plagued Colombia during the 1980s to solidify his control over the Medellín cartel and the country's cocaine trade.

By funding left-wing terrorist groups, killing his enemies and sponsoring attempts at regime change, Escobar was able to set rival forces against one another to his advantage.

While some may romanticize kingpins such as El Chapo and Pablo Escobar into counterculture figureheads, it is important to fully understand the breadth of their crimes: the bombing of civilian targets; the execution of politicians and law enforcement officials; the assassination of witnesses and their families. Then there is the larger human cost: Thousands of men, women and children in the United States perish every year as a direct result of drug addiction. In Bogotá, for every fond memory of Escobar's philanthropy toward the city's poor, there are many more recollections of the countless public bombings in the same city carried out by the Medellín cartel. Drug kingpins leave an indelible mark on the communities they use for narcotrafficking, and their far-reaching impact can take years to undo by even the most vigilant law enforcement efforts.

CHAPTER 1

The Crimes of El Chapo

When one considers the illicit world of drugs today, the most notorious name is "El Chapo." The life of Joaquín Archivaldo Guzmán Loera is well-documented in his native Mexico, and in the rest of North America his reputation has afforded him celebrity-like status. His many escapes from Mexican prisons read like Wild-West myths. As the leader of the Sinaloa cartel, El Chapo ordered the deaths of his rivals. Indeed, El Chapo was a household name long before he was convicted in Brooklyn for drug trafficking and murder.

Searching for El Chapo From the Sports Desk

TIMES INSIDER | BY RANDY ARCHIBOLD | JULY 15, 2015

Times Insider delivers behind-the-scenes insights into how news, features and opinion come together at The New York Times.

FROM MY DESK, I caught snippets of conversation that affect my new job as deputy sports editor in The Times's New York office. A columnist discussed plans for a future column with an editor; off in the distance, the name of retired baseball commissioner Bud Selig hung in the air after being uttered in another conservation. On a big-screen television tuned to ESPN, something about Dez Bryant and a contract flicked by.

But my focus was far afield my first day on the new job, which I began Monday after five years as the bureau chief for Mexico, Central America and the Caribbean.

The phone rang. It was my former editor Greg Winter, on the international desk. He wanted to talk about Joaquín Guzmán Loera, the infamous Mexican drug lord better known as El Chapo, who had escaped last weekend in made-for-TV-movie fashion through a tunnel bored under the country's most secure prison.

It is common for correspondents to switch jobs after several years in the field. Changing jobs, not to mention moving from one country to another, often comes with its share of bumps. One is the possibility of breaking news yanking you back to your old job.

As a friend jokingly said, "You can check out, but you can never leave."

In the case of Chapo's escape it was all hands — old and new — on deck.

Damien Cave, now a deputy national editor who served as a correspondent with me in Mexico for several years, joined in from New York, teaming up with my successor in the Mexico bureau, Azam Ahmed, on another story. William Neuman, the Andean-region bureau chief based in Caracas who was fresh from covering the Pope's visit to South America, flew to Mexico to help.

I was sitting in my sister-in-law's TV room in suburban New York, preparing for a day of relative relaxation before starting my new job, when the old job came knocking, or rather pinging. An editor forwarded an email copy of the Associated Press report on El Chapo's escape.

A hoax, I initially thought. Could Chapo really be that daring?

He could, and the desk called in short order, sending me and Elisabeth Malkin, a mainstay in the Mexico bureau who happened to be on vacation, and Azam to cover the breaking news.

I hadn't made it to the office or my new desk in the sports department before the international desk called again, to ask my help for the day's follow-up story.

It can be disorienting to think ahead and back at the same time. As I thumbed through phone numbers and email addresses from Mexico and made calls, members of my new staff dropped by my desk to welcome me. I was invited to a sports desk story meeting right around the time the international desk was calling to discuss the approach for the Mexico story.

Sources were confused also as I explained by phone that, yes, I left Mexico and was in New York but, well, it's Chapo!

Naturally, jokes came easily too, given that my arrival coincided with his escape. "Was he in your trunk?" asked more than a few colleagues. "Find Chapo yet?" others called out.

But in the end I relished joining in on such a big, important story that says much about Mexico's chronic problems with crime, rule of law, corruption and institutional failure. We carry many titles at The Times, but at bottom we are all journalists who love a good story.

Now, on to that Dez Bryant story.

El Chapo, Escaped Mexican Drug Lord, Is Recaptured in Gun Battle

BY AZAM AHMED | JAN. 8, 2016

MEXICO CITY — He became a byword for government incompetence, a figure who seemed invincible after he burrowed his way out of the country's most secure prison.

But on Friday, nearly six months after his escape, Joaquín Guzmán Loera, the Mexican drug lord known as El Chapo, was captured again after a fierce gun battle near the coast in his home state, Sinaloa, Mexican officials said. "Mission accomplished: We have him," President Enrique Peña Nieto announced.

The arrest ended one of the most extensive manhunts undertaken by the government, involving every law enforcement agency in the country and help from the United States.

But it was the marines, Mexico's most-trusted military force, who managed to capture the fugitive in an early morning raid that left five people dead, the Mexican authorities said. An American official also described the raid as "a Mexican op, planned and executed by Mexico."

The government said late Friday that Mr. Guzmán had been planning a movie about his life and that his people had been in contact with actors and producers, which had allowed the authorities to track him down. It said that the authorities had been watching a home in Los Mochis for more than a month when law enforcement officers finally saw movement on Thursday. Officials said that during the ensuing raid, Mr. Guzmán managed to slip away through the sewers, and then he surfaced, stole a car and was apprehended. The authorities took him to a hotel to wait for backup.

The capture of the drug lord concludes a deeply embarrassing chapter for the government of Mr. Peña Nieto, which has been waylaid by a series of security and corruption scandals that reached their low point with Mr. Guzmán's daring escape.

Now, a looming question is whether the Mexican authorities will try to hold Mr. Guzmán for a third time — he has already escaped from prison twice — or whether they will hand him over to the Americans.

Mexican officials are busily debating the issue. Some are arguing for a "fast-track" extradition that could put him in the United States quickly, while others want to continue a previous process that could take months, according to two people with knowledge of the discussions. Mr. Guzmán, the head of Mexico's most powerful cartel, is facing indictments in at least seven American federal courts on charges that include narcotics trafficking and murder.

With operations that span much of Mexico, his organization has specialized in smuggling tons of drugs into the United States through vast networks of tunnels deep beneath the border. His success has made him among the richest drug dealers in history: Forbes magazine estimated his net worth at close to $1 billion.

Mr. Guzmán stunned the world last summer when he stepped into the shower in his cell, in the most secure wing of the prison, and abruptly vanished in full view of a video camera. Guards later discovered a small hole in the shower floor.

It led to a mile-long tunnel to a construction site. The tunnel was tall enough for Mr. Guzmán to walk through standing upright — his nickname translates to Shorty — and had been dug more than 30 feet underground. It was equipped with lighting, ventilation and a motorcycle on rails. Some engineers estimated that the tunnel took more than a year and at least $1 million to build.

The prison break humiliated the government of Mr. Peña Nieto, which had proclaimed the arrests of Mr. Guzmán and the leaders of other drug cartels as crucial achievements in restoring order and sovereignty to a country long beleaguered by the horrific violence associated with organized crime. It was particularly embarrassing because Mr. Guzmán had already escaped from prison in 2001, when his conspirators managed to smuggle him out. By some accounts, he escaped that time by hiding in a laundry bin.

There are still major questions ahead, including the potential extradition of Mr. Guzmán to the United States. Shortly after Mr. Guzmán was captured in 2014, the attorney general of Mexico at the time refused to extradite him to the United States, saying that the criminal would serve his time in Mexico first before he was sent to another country.

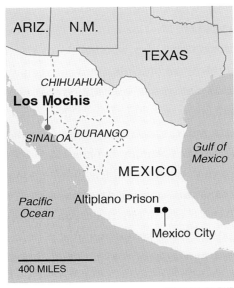

Officials and analysts said it was an effort to show sovereignty and put some distance between the Mexican authorities and their American counterparts, who often used a heavy hand to influence policy in Mexico.

But that stance came to haunt the Peña Nieto administration after the kingpin escaped. The United States had issued a formal request for his extradition less than three weeks before Mr. Guzmán broke out.

A few months later, the Mexican government extradited several top drug lords to the United States, suggesting a new spirit of cooperation in the wake of Mr. Guzmán's escape. The people extradited included an American citizen, Edgar Valdez Villarreal, a notorious figure known as "La Barbie," as well as people charged with participating in the murders of a United States Consulate worker and an American immigration and customs agent.

While the likelihood that Mr. Guzmán could escape from an American maximum security prison is considered low, extradition would still come at a cost to the image of the Mexican state, some analysts say. "Extraditing him is a way to say we cannot cope with this with our own institutions," said Pablo A. Piccato, a history professor at Columbia University. "While this is something everyone knows, obviously the government has not been able to publicly recognize this or tackle it in the past."

Several senior politicians from Mr. Peña Nieto's party were already calling for extradition, including Emilio Gamboa, the head of the governing party in the Senate, who told local news media that he agreed with the idea.

In a statement on Friday, the American attorney general, Loretta E. Lynch, commended the Mexican authorities "who have worked tirelessly in recent months to bring Guzmán to justice." But she did not directly answer the extradition question.

The Justice Department "is proud to maintain a close and effective relationship with our Mexican counterparts, and we look forward to continuing our work together to ensure the safety and security of all our people," she said.

In the aftermath of Mr. Guzmán's escape last July, American officials were frustrated with what they considered Mexico's resistance to accepting help in the manhunt. After his escape, American officials offered to give their Mexican counterparts whatever assistance they could.

When Mexico rebuffed the offer, many officials in both countries worried that Mr. Guzmán might never be caught.

In October, security forces said they had located Mr. Guzmán in the remote northwestern mountains where he had been hiding out, an area known as the Golden Triangle at the border of his home state of Sinaloa, Durango and Chihuahua. After a gun battle, officials said, he escaped, with wounds to his face and leg.

The authorities ultimately captured Mr. Guzmán in Los Mochis, a coastal town of about 250,000 people that has long been known as a center of boxing in Mexico.

"People knew he would be caught any time; the government was going after him hard," said Adrián Cabrera, a blogger in Culiacán, the capital of Sinaloa, adding that Mr. Guzmán was still a popular figure in Sinaloa.

"The new corridos will start coming out pretty soon," Mr. Cabrera said, referring to the songs often used to glorify the exploits of local drug traffickers. "He's from here. He has a lot of sympathy here. It's his turf."

When Mr. Guzmán was finally recaptured, the president broke the news himself, via Twitter. Given his sagging popularity — his ratings are the lowest of any president in the last 25 years — Mr. Peña Nieto seemed eager to declare the success personally.

In a statement on Friday, Mr. Peña Nieto said that the arrest was the culmination of months of work, an example of Mexico's ability to overcome adversity. "Our security institutions have demonstrated that our citizens can trust them and that they have the stature, strength and determination to accomplish any mission they are tasked with," Mr. Peña Nieto said.

Mr. Guzmán's lawyers have already filed legal injunctions against his extradition to the United States. Wherever he ends up, few people here think that his capture will change much for the government's popularity, life for Mexicans or the strength of the Sinaloa cartel. "This won't have much effect on their internal structure," said Eduardo Guerrero, a Mexico City-based security analyst. "They are prepared for this kind of news. They probably even have a protocol for it."

Reporting was contributed by **NICHOLAS CASEY** and **WILLIAM NEUMAN** from Caracas, Venezuela; **DAMIEN CAVE** from New York; **ERIC LICHTBLAU** from Washington; and **ELISABETH MALKIN** and **PAULINA VILLEGAS** from Mexico City.

How Rolling Stone Handled Ramifications of El Chapo Exclusive

BY RAVI SOMAIYA | JAN. 10, 2016

SEVERAL MONTHS AGO, Jann Wenner, a founder of Rolling Stone magazine, received a call from the actor Sean Penn.

Mr. Penn, Mr. Wenner said in an interview on Sunday, wanted to discuss something important. But he did not want to speak openly over the phone, so the two began to speak elliptically about a potential project.

That vague conversation was the beginning of what eventually became an article, written by Mr. Penn, that rocked both Mexico and the United States when it was published Saturday night. It was an exclusive interview with Joaquín Guzmán Loera, the notorious drug kingpin known as El Chapo, that was conducted while Mr. Guzmán was on the run from the authorities after an audacious escape from a Mexican prison last year.

The 10,000-word article includes accusations of cooperation between the military and Mr. Guzmán's Sinaloa cartel, as well as Mr. Guzmán's acknowledgment of his status as a drug dealer and his thoughts about the ethical implications of his business. Mr. Guzmán, whose escape from prison — his second — made him one of the most wanted fugitives in the world, was caught on Friday, before the article was published.

But after its publication, questions have been raised about the ethics for the magazine in dealing with Mr. Guzmán, a criminal being sought on charges of drug trafficking and murder, and in allowing him to approve what would ultimately be published about him. The Republican presidential candidate Marco Rubio, speaking Sunday on "This Week," on ABC News, acknowledged Mr. Penn's "constitutional right" to meet with Mr. Guzmán, but called the interview "grotesque."

Steve Coll, the dean of the Columbia University Graduate School of Journalism, said he was concerned by the editorial approval offered to Mr. Guzmán. But ultimately, he said, "scoring an exclusive interview with a wanted criminal is legitimate journalism no matter who the reporter is."

Mr. Wenner said that he did not think it was plausible that the magazine would become embroiled in the legal case against Mr. Guzmán. "They got their man, so what do they need us for?" he said. "There is nothing we can add anymore."

After Mr. Penn and Mr. Wenner agreed to pursue the article, Mr. Wenner said Rolling Stone strove for secrecy. In early October, he said, he was unable to reach Mr. Penn for a number of days. When Mr. Penn next contacted Mr. Wenner, he said that he had met with Mr. Guzmán, as they had discussed previously. That meeting also included Kate del Castillo, a Mexican actress who once played a drug kingpin on a soap opera. "It was just between me and Sean, for a couple of weeks as he wrote his draft," Mr. Wenner said.

A lawyer for the magazine, and its managing editor, Jason Fine, were eventually brought in to help with the editing process. Work on the article was completed about two weeks ago, Mr. Wenner said, but because of Rolling Stone's production cycle, those involved were subjected to an excruciating wait for the next issue, during which time Mr. Guzmán was captured.

The reporting and editing of the article were closely held, in part, to avoid the authorities. "I was worried that I did not want to provide the details that would be responsible for his capture," Mr. Wenner said. "We were very conscientious on our end and on Sean's end, keeping it quiet, using a separate protected part of our server for emails."

Around Thanksgiving, as Mr. Penn negotiated with Mr. Guzmán and his intermediaries to include a video component of the interview, which was eventually sent to him by courier, the magazine was convinced that it would have to resist pressure from the authorities in the

United States and Mexico who would want to learn as much as they could about Mr. Guzmán's whereabouts.

"We made sure we didn't have any information to give them, other than what we published," he said. "But we would have done everything that a traditional journalism operation would have done in terms of protecting sources."

Mr. Wenner said that Mr. Guzmán seemed to have become careless with those he contacted while on the run, and would most likely have been tracked whether or not Mr. Penn wrote an article. In fact, the meeting between Mr. Guzmán and Mr. Penn had been monitored by the authorities, according to a Mexican official with knowledge of the operation. That led to an October raid on Mr. Guzmán's compound in the state of Durango in which he managed to evade capture but which gave the authorities more intelligence about his movements.

The article was edited by Mr. Wenner and Mr. Fine, with Mr. Fine responsible for the final line editing before publication. Responding to criticisms of the piece's distinctive writing style, which was mocked on social media, and its discursions into topics including flatulence and technology, Mr. Fine said: "It's a piece by Sean Penn. Sean Penn has a particular style and point of view, and I'm happy with it."

Mr. Penn has not commented publicly since the article was published.

Mr. Fine said that he, too, had considered the ethics involved with the article's publication and the magazine's arrangement with its subject. If Mr. Guzmán wanted changes, he said, the magazine had the option of not publishing the piece.

There is a long history of journalists interviewing subjects who were either on the run from the authorities or who were considered unsavory for other reasons. Osama bin Laden was interviewed through the late 1990s, after he had declared jihad on the United States (though before the Sept. 11 attacks). In 2013, the former basketball star Dennis Rodman went to North Korea to meet with that country's repressive dictator, Kim Jong-un, for Vice.

As for giving Mr. Guzmán final approval over the article, Mr. Wenner said: "I don't think it was a meaningful thing in the first place. We have let people in the past approve their quotes in interviews."

Mr. Guzmán, he said, did not speak English and seemed to have little interest in editing Mr. Penn's work. "In this case, it was a small thing to do in exchange for what we got," Mr. Wenner said.

Still, critics of Rolling Stone remain unconvinced. Andrew Seaman, the chair of the ethics committee for the Society of Professional Journalists, wrote in a blog post that "allowing any source control over a story's content is inexcusable."

The practice of pre-approval, he said, "discredits the entire story — whether the subject requests changes or not. The writer, who in this case is an actor and activist, may write the story in a more favorable light and omit unflattering facts in an attempt to not be rejected."

Mr. Coll agreed that the offer of preapproval was wrong. But, he said, "It's hard to judge what Rolling Stone was thinking since apparently the veto wasn't exercised, freeing the magazine of any dilemma."

For the magazine, Mr. Wenner said, the interview with El Chapo represented a welcome turn. It was believed to be the first interview Mr. Guzmán had granted in decades.

Last year, Rolling Stone was heavily criticized for a discredited article that alleged a brutal gang rape had taken place at the University of Virginia. After publication, the police, and people close to that situation, questioned the article's veracity.

A report commissioned by Rolling Stone in the wake of the controversy over the article, and co-authored by Mr. Coll, concluded that the rape article was the result of failures at every stage of the reporting and editing process. The magazine retracted the article and became the subject of lawsuits filed on the matter.

Of Mr. Penn's article, which was subject to follow-up interviews with eyewitnesses for fact-checking, Mr. Wenner said, "It's not a vindication but a restatement of how good we are, how strong we are."

AZAM AHMED contributed reporting.

El Chapo, Mexican Drug Kingpin, Is Extradited to U.S.

BY AZAM AHMED | JAN. 19, 2017

MEXICO CITY — Joaquín Guzmán Loera, the notorious drug lord known as El Chapo who twice slipped out of high-security Mexican prisons and into criminal legend, was extradited to the United States on Thursday night, officials said, drawing to a close a decades-long quest to prosecute the head of one of the world's largest narcotics organizations.

A federal court in Mexico denied an appeal by Mr. Guzmán's lawyers to block the extradition, clearing the way for his transfer to the American authorities in New York, where he faces numerous charges for his role as the chieftain of the Sinaloa cartel. Mr. Guzmán was put on a plane on Thursday in Ciudad Juárez, near the border with Texas, and arrived in the United States on President Obama's final night in office.

According to a Justice Department statement late Thursday, he was flown to Long Island MacArthur Airport in Islip, N.Y.

The decision to extradite Mr. Guzmán was an about-face for the Mexican government, which once claimed that he would serve his long sentence in Mexico first. However, after his Houdini-like escape in 2015, when his associates tunneled him out of Mexico's most secure prison, officials began to reconsider.

When he was recaptured early last year, after one of Mexico's most exhaustive manhunts, the government publicly said it would allow the extradition of Mr. Guzmán, thus relieving itself of the potential embarrassment of another escape and preventing further souring of its relationship with the United States.

Mr. Guzmán's extradition came suddenly, after nearly a year of appeals and legal procedures. Even his own lawyer was surprised. In an interview after the announcement by the Mexican government, the lawyer, José Refugio Rodríguez, said he had only just learned about the extradition. Indeed, he was at the prison where Mr. Guzmán was being held, planning to see his client, when it was locked down for two hours.

"I was supposed to visit him today," he said. "I know nothing of this."

An American law enforcement official said the United States authorities had not known that the Mexicans were about to hand over Mr. Guzmán until late Thursday afternoon. The official, who requested anonymity to discuss the case, said the "guesstimate" was that the timing of the extradition was "politically motivated." The official did not elaborate.

Mr. Guzmán — whose nickname, El Chapo, means "Shorty" — was a major trophy for law enforcement officials in both countries. Over the years, as the drug trade blossomed into a multibillion-dollar industry, he became much more than a mere trafficker. As a farm-boy-turned-billionaire with a flair for the dramatic, he became a symbol of Mexico's broken rule of law, America's narcotics obsession and the failure of both nations' drug wars.

And yet, amid the anguish caused by Mr. Guzmán — the trail of blood left by his henchmen across swaths of Mexico; the addiction crisis fueled by his networks in America — his legend only seemed to grow. In Mexico, he became a folk hero to the masses. In Sinaloa, tales of Mr. Guzmán's handing out freebies to the poor and covering checks for diners in the restaurants he frequented are commonplace.

But his daring escapes cemented his reputation as an outlaw.

Mr. Guzmán first managed to break out of a prison in 2001 — according to some accounts, by hiding in a laundry cart. In the ensuing years, while on the run, he seemed always just out of the grasp of the authorities, slipping into secret passages beneath bathtubs or absconding seconds before federal raids.

The fascination with Mr. Guzmán stemmed from the fact that one could never really count him out. He perfected the escape hatch, the underground tunnel and the trap door — all tools he used to evade law enforcement during his years on the run, which ended with an arrest in 2014. He sent his engineers to Germany for training, then dispatched them to his homes, where they would outfit closets, bathrooms and refrigerators with secret exits.

A pioneer of the cross-border tunnel, used to shuttle tens of thousands of tons of drugs into America, he ultimately adapted those feats of secret underground engineering for his escape from the Altiplano prison: a maximum-security facility in the State of Mexico where he lived in isolation, under 24-hour surveillance by a camera in his cell.

On the night of July 11, 2015, shortly before 9 p.m., Mr. Guzmán stepped into his shower and passed through a small hole in its floor, positioned in the camera's one blind spot. From there, he descended into a mile-long tunnel, equipped with a motorcycle on rails, and raced to freedom.

His escape was a stinging embarrassment for the government of President Enrique Peña Nieto, which had trumpeted his capture as a crucial victory in its bloody campaign against the narcotics trade.

Again a fugitive, Mr. Guzmán found the time to rendezvous with film stars, including Sean Penn, to discuss a biopic about his life. But his freedom was short-lived. After a manhunt that involved more than 2,500 people, he was seized in the town of Los Mochis in early 2016 after crawling out of a sewer.

Once he was back in prison, many worried that he would escape once more, prompting the authorities to rotate him from cell to cell and, eventually, to send him up north, to the border with Texas.

The general belief is that, in the United States, El Chapo's antics will be much harder to pull off. Though his reputation may not diminish, his chances of escape, or acquittal, are drastically lower there, experts say.

Mr. Guzmán faces charges stemming from six separate indictments in the United States. In the Eastern District of New York in Brooklyn, where he is expected to face prosecution, he is charged with the manufacture and distribution of a range of drugs, the use of fire-arms, money laundering and running an ongoing criminal enterprise. The indictment, first filed in 2009, has been updated three times since then.

In a statement on Thursday night, the United States Justice Department said it extended "its gratitude to the government of Mexico for their extensive cooperation and assistance in securing the extradition of Guzmán Loera to the United States."

In ridding itself of Mr. Guzmán, the Mexican government has lifted at least one giant weight from its shoulders: that of keeping and successfully prosecuting the notorious escape artist. He is departing, however, at a time of deep political unrest in the country, as protests over an increase in gasoline prices continue and corruption scandals, as well as rising crime, nag at the nation's image.

The American president-elect, Donald J. Trump, has made threatening Mexico over trade and immigration a center of his platform. It is unclear whether the decision to extradite Mr. Guzmán the day before Mr. Trump's inauguration was connected in any way with the hostile tone the president-elect has adopted toward Mexico.

"The fact that we delivered him to Obama is a clear political message that says this is a government we have long collaborated and worked closely with," said Jorge Chabat, an expert on security at CIDE, a Mexico City research institution. "By not waiting to send him to Trump after his inauguration, it is a subtle statement saying, 'We could do this for you, too, in the future, if we have a good relationship.' "

"If not, there won't be any other powerful narco traffickers extra-dited," he said.

WILLIAM K. RASHBAUM contributed reporting from New York, and **PAULINA VILLEGAS** from Mexico City.

The U.S. Case vs. El Chapo: 10,000 Pages and Recordings

BY ALAN FEUER | MAY 5, 2017

IT HAS BEEN ASSUMED for months that the prosecution of Joaquín Guzmán Loera, the Mexican drug lord known as El Chapo, would be an undertaking of major proportions.

At the news conference in January when the charges against him were announced, federal prosecutors described a Shakespearean cast of more than 40 witnesses who would testify that, over three decades, Mr. Guzmán had built the world's biggest drug empire, employing an army of assassins and earning billions of dollars by trafficking his product with a rotating fleet of trucks, planes, fishing boats, submersibles and yachts.

But on Friday, the true scope of the case came into view, and the details suggest it is going to be enormous. At a hearing in Federal District Court in Brooklyn, prosecutors said that Mr. Guzmán's trial could last three months and include up to 1,500 audio recordings of the defendant and his allies alongside nearly 10,000 pages of documents. The presiding judge, Brian M. Cogan, set what he called an "aspirational" trial date: April 2018.

The sweeping nature of the case, which will track Mr. Guzmán's rise from a teenage marijuana farmer to an international kingpin who carried a diamond-encrusted pistol, is matched by his outsize reputation. The United States attorney's office in Brooklyn has portrayed him not only as the world's most sophisticated drug dealer, but also as a coldblooded killer who ordered the deaths of thousands of people during Mexico's brutal drug wars.

Mr. Guzmán is still considered something of a folk hero in his homeland, not least for having twice escaped from high-security prisons there, the first time in a laundry cart and later by way of a mile-long tunnel dug into the shower of his cell.

It was hard to reconcile either of those images with the unimposing figure that Mr. Guzmán cut in court on Friday. He is a small man — El Chapo means Shorty in Spanish — and spent much of the hourlong hearing staring into space while following a translation of the proceedings through headphones.

Only two things seemed to engage his distracted attention: his wife, Emma Coronel Aispuro, a former beauty queen who sat in the gallery in a crisp white blazer, and the numerous court security guards, at whom he occasionally cast fleeting glances.

The primary subject of the hearing was an argument over whether Mr. Guzmán's lawyers, the federal defenders Michelle Gelernt and Michael Schneider, could continue to represent him. The government has said the two have a conflict of interest because other lawyers in their office had, in the past, briefly represented two prosecution witnesses who were preparing to testify at trial.

Judge Cogan, saying the matter was "barely an issue," ruled that the lawyers could remain in place.

Ms. Gelernt and Mr. Schneider have argued for several weeks that Mr. Guzmán is suffering the ill effects of being held in almost constant isolation in what is known as 10 South, the most secure wing of the Metropolitan Correctional Center, a federal jail in Lower Manhattan across the river from the Brooklyn court.

On Thursday, Judge Cogan issued an order rejecting nearly all of the defense's requests to ease the restrictions that have been imposed on Mr. Guzmán. The measures were necessary, the judge wrote, to keep the defendant from running his former operation, the Sinaloa drug cartel, while he was being held.

The judge's decision did not stop Ms. Gelernt from complaining again on Friday that the terms of Mr. Guzmán's confinement had made it almost impossible to prepare him for trial. She told Judge Cogan that she and Mr. Schneider were not, for instance, allowed to be in the same room at the jail as their client. If they wanted to show him a document, she said, they had to hold it up to a plexiglass window between them.

This appeared to disturb Judge Cogan, who called the process "cumbersome." Looking down from his bench, he asked the prosecutors, "How are we going to get this case ready for trial if they have to do that?"

When the prosecutors could not provide a response, Judge Cogan offered his own: A junior judge would be sent to 10 South to investigate more efficient options. He added that "in the interest of moving things along," this would happen soon.

In El Chapo's Trial, Extraordinary Steps to Keep Witnesses Alive

BY ALAN FEUER | OCT. 1, 2018

INTERNATIONAL DRUG LORDS sometimes kill people who plan to take the witness stand against them. It has happened so often in Mexico, for example, that some have described the country's witness protection program as a witness detection program, or a hit list.

As the authorities in New York prepare for the trial next month of the world's most famous drug lord — Joaquín Guzmán Loera, who is best known as El Chapo — they have taken extraordinary steps to keep those who will testify from getting killed. Mr. Guzmán's lawyers say those strict protective orders have made mounting a strong defense more challenging.

Here are few of the ways the prosecution has kept the witnesses, and issues at the trial that concern them, under a veil of secrecy, and why:

SHIELDING NAMES ON COURT DOCUMENTS

From the moment Mr. Guzmán was extradited to Brooklyn from Mexico last year, prosecutors have argued that he presents an "extreme danger" to the numerous former allies, rivals and underlings who will ultimately testify against him.

The government has repeatedly refused to identify the witnesses in any public papers, saying that if it does, the Sinaloa drug cartel, which Mr. Guzmán ran for 20 years, could easily seek revenge.

Late last month, for example, when the government provided basic information on the witnesses to Mr. Guzmán's lawyers, it did so in a 100-page memo, almost half of which was blacked out by redactions. Secrecy has so suffused the case that when the defense responded to the memo three days later, asking to learn more about the witnesses, the document was filed under seal.

The chief complaint by Mr. Guzmán's lawyer, A. Eduardo Balarezo, is that the government is planning to withhold the witnesses' identities until the eve of trial. He has argued that doing so will hinder his ability to investigate their claims and devise a defense against them.

KEEPING WITNESSES HEAVILY PROTECTED

Some of the government's witnesses are already in jail and are being held in what are known as protective custody units "in light of the great risk to their lives," according to court papers. Others are in the witness protection program in undisclosed locations and have been given new identities. Under the program's rules, the papers say, those individuals have been told "to cut off all ties with family and friends in order to maintain the highest levels of protection."

Prosecutors have also had concerns about safety of the jury in the case. Earlier this year, they persuaded a federal judge, Brian M. Cogan, to allow the jurors to serve anonymously.

Judge Cogan decided to select the jurors in a rare closed session conducted in his private chambers.

PREPARING FOR WHAT COULD HAPPEN

Strict protective orders of witnesses are necessary because Mr. Guzmán has a history of killing and kidnapping those who have dared to speak against him, prosecutors said. It has been difficult, however, to verify the government's allegations because, as with so many aspects of the case, they were made in documents filed under seal.

In October 2016, Vicente Bermúdez Zacarías, a Mexican judge who played a role in Mr. Guzmán's extradition battle, went for a jog in his hometown, Metepec, when a man shot him in the head.

In 2009, prosecutors say, the father of two men from Chicago who were cooperating against Mr. Guzmán with American authorities was captured and murdered when he was in Mexico.

In the Brooklyn case, Mr. Guzmán has been accused of ordering the deaths of thousands as he ran the cartel. That is on top of charges that he smuggled more than 200 tons of cocaine into the United States.

Before his extradition, Mr. Guzmán also escaped two times from prisons in Mexico in a pair of daring jailbreaks.

ISOLATING EL CHAPO

Despite all this, Mr. Guzmán's lawyers have dismissed the notion that he presents a threat to anyone given that he has spent the past two years in what is called 10 South, the maximum-security wing of the Metropolitan Correctional Center, New York City's most impenetrable jail.

There he has been under lock and key, except for an hour a day. He is permitted visits only from his lawyers and his 7-year-old daughters. Every month, Mr. Guzmán is allowed two 15-minutes phone calls with his mother and his sister, to which the government is listening. Other than that, he is "completely isolated from the world outside of his dismal cell," wrote Mr. Balarezo last month.

Considering those "extremely restrictive conditions," Mr. Balarezo has claimed it is impossible for Mr. Guzmán to get word out to his associates to knock off any witnesses.

"In fact," he recently wrote, "unless the government is suggesting that the defense team will disseminate hit orders from Mr. Guzmán, there is no realistic way for him to do anything" to the witnesses at all.

Prosecutors' Plan for El Chapo: Tie Him to 33 Killings

BY ALAN FEUER | OCT. 30, 2018

EVEN GIVEN THE HISTORY of Mexico's bloody drug wars, it was startling this month when federal prosecutors said they planned to offer evidence that Joaquín Guzmán Loera, the longtime leader of the Sinaloa drug cartel, had taken part in no less than 33 murders.

That number was high enough that on Tuesday the judge presiding over his trial in Brooklyn called it "way too much" and "out of control."

Apparently exasperated at the prospect of testimony about so many slayings, the judge, Brian M. Cogan, told the government that it hardly needed to detail every murder that Mr. Guzmán, who is known as El Chapo, is suspected of committing to make its point that he used violence to run his operation.

Judge Cogan also warned the prosecution that if its presentation got too gory, he might cut it short.

"This is a drug conspiracy case that involves murders," Judge Cogan said at a hearing in Federal District Court in Brooklyn. "I'm not going to let you try a murder conspiracy case that happens to involve drugs.

"Take your best shot and cut the rest," he added.

Among the victims the jury will likely hear about is Israel Rincón Martínez, a member of a rival cartel who was targeted in 2010, court papers say, after killing the son of one of Mr. Guzmán's closest allies.

Prosecutors are also expected to describe the execution of Francisco Aceves Urías, a Guzmán gunman known as Barbarino, who was slain in 2015 in the parking lot of a restaurant in Culiacán, Mexico.

Brutal as they are, the 33 killings Mr. Guzmán stands accused of do not reflect the full scope of the bloodshed that prosecutors plan to introduce at his trial, which starts on Monday with jury selection. They are also poised to describe how the defendant killed — or ordered the deaths of — an untold number of law enforcement officers and people who betrayed him.

Everything about the Guzmán case has been supersized. Though the defendant's nickname means "Shorty" in Spanish, he is a towering figure described in court papers as the greatest criminal of the 21st century.

Hundreds of thousands of photographs and documents are likely to be introduced at his trial. At least 16 cooperating witnesses — mostly former underlings and rivals — are expected to appear on the witness stand and testify against him.

Facing this onslaught, Mr. Guzmán's lawyers have spent the last few weeks complaining to Judge Cogan that there is no way for them to digest the pile of evidence arrayed against their client and successfully defend him.

Earlier this month, they filed a motion accusing the government of inundating them with 117,000 audio recordings and 14,000 new pages of documents. To show how buried in paperwork they were, the lawyers brought the documents to court Tuesday morning and lined them up in 23 white plastic binders, stacked, one next to the other, on a table.

But Judge Cogan refused their request to delay the trial again. (It has already been adjourned two times.) He also bemoaned that the defense and prosecution seemed to be in state of high anxiety, peppering him with last-minute requests and pestering him with "panicked" phone calls, sometimes on weekends.

He asked both sides to settle down and implored them to lessen the tension.

"I don't think litigating by frenzy and hysteria is an appropriate way to approach this case," he said.

Wanted: 12 People Willing to Serve as Jurors in El Chapo Trial

BY ALAN FEUER | NOV. 5, 2018

WANTED: TWELVE PEOPLE who can take four months off work and who don't mind sitting in judgment of a man said to be the most notorious criminal of the 21st century. Payment: About $40 a day.

Picking a jury is always hard, but it is even more so when the defendant on trial is Joaquín Guzmán Loera, the former head of the Sinaloa drug cartel, a man accused of trafficking drugs by the ton and of having a hand in at least 30 murders.

Mr. Guzmán — known to the world as El Chapo — is such a fearsome figure that earlier this year, the judge in the case ruled that the jury would remain anonymous and would be escorted for their safety to and from the court each day by United States Marshals.

Still, as jury selection started Monday in Federal District Court in Brooklyn, it was largely smooth sailing as the potential jurors seemed to evince little fear of the man who sat across from them, silent but watchful, in a navy blue suit and a crisp white shirt that was open to his sternum.

Amid questions about their views on marijuana, their feelings about law enforcement and their fluency in Spanish, only one said that she was afraid of Mr. Guzmán. Another admitted that the words "El Chapo" mostly made him think about a bagel sandwich served by a deli near his workplace that was named for the defendant. A third spent most of his time as he was questioned talking about his job as a Michael Jackson impersonator.

Many of the jurors said they recognized Mr. Guzmán's name and had at least heard that he was an international kingpin who had famously escaped from two Mexican prisons. Of the 46 people questioned on Monday by Judge Brian M. Cogan, 17 were dismissed, most of them because they said they could not be fair to Mr. Guzmán or because the long trial would cause a financial hardship.

Joaquín Guzmán Loera, the Mexican drug lord known as El Chapo, arriving at Long Island MacArthur Airport in January 2017. Jury selection began in his trial on Monday.

Security was exceedingly tight. The courthouse was guarded by marshals, local court officers, a bomb-sniffing dog and a heavily armed tactical team of New York City police officers. Precautions like these apparently unnerved one potential juror, who admitted that the prospect of deciding Mr. Guzmán's fate made her feel "unsafe."

"What scares me is I read that his family will come after jurors and their families," the woman said. She added that she knew that Mr. Guzmán had two sons who were still at large. When a defense lawyer asked her if that made her nervous, she admitted that it did.

Several prospective jurors said they were familiar with Mr. Guzmán from the Netflix series "El Chapo" or had seen his page on Wikipedia, but they seemed largely unaware that he had been charged almost a decade ago with running a criminal enterprise that smuggled cocaine and heroin into the United States from Mexico in a rotating fleet of cars, trucks, yachts, planes and submarines. Mr. Guzmán also stands accused of protecting his empire by murdering — or ordering the deaths of — dozens of people.

Opening arguments are scheduled to begin next Tuesday, assuming a jury has been picked. Prosecutors are expected to offer up the epic tale of Mr. Guzmán's rise from a teenage marijuana farmer to a ruthless kingpin who bribed officials in Mexico and often toted a gold-plated assault rifle. The jury will also likely hear about his two daring jailbreaks — one, at least according to lore, while hidden in a laundry cart and the other through a mile-long tunnel his associates dug into the shower of his cell.

But the sobering facts at the heart of the case did not preclude jury selection from veering at times into the absurd. There was, after all, the juror who noted that his local deli had a sandwich called the "El Chapo."

William Purpura, one of Mr. Guzmán's lawyers, wanted to explore this coincidence, asking what precisely the sandwich was made of. It was, as it turned out, a bagel with cream cheese, capers and lox, the man explained.

"I don't know why it's called the 'El Chapo,' " he said, "but it's delicious."

El Chapo's Defense: He Was Framed by Vast Conspiracy

BY ALAN FEUER AND EMILY PALMER | NOV. 13, 2018

LAWYERS FOR JOAQUÍN GUZMÁN LOERA, the infamous drug lord known as El Chapo, claimed on Tuesday that for decades their client had been framed by a vast conspiracy of plotters, including his chief lieutenant in the Sinaloa cartel, American drug agents, and the last two presidents of Mexico.

The defense's claim was an unexpected start to Mr. Guzmán's drug conspiracy trial, which after several delays on Tuesday began under tight security in Federal District Court in Brooklyn.

During an impassioned opening statement, one of Mr. Guzmán's lawyers, Jeffrey Lichtman, said that the real mastermind of the cartel, which Mr. Guzmán has been accused of running for decades, was his longtime partner Ismael Zambada García.

Describing Mr. Guzmán as no more than "a scapegoat," Mr. Lichtman argued that Mr. Zambada, known as El Mayo, had been the one to oversee 20 years of drug shipments into the United States, and who repeatedly paid off — to the tune of millions of dollars — a "completely corrupt" Mexican government, including top officials like President Enrique Peña Nieto and his predecessor, Felipe Calderón.

"The world is focusing on this mythical El Chapo creature," Mr. Lichtman said. "The world is not focusing on Mayo Zambada."

Mr. Zambada, 70, has long been one of Mr. Guzmán's closest deputies and is believed to be still at large in Mexico. Though he has been never been arrested, he was named as a defendant in the same 2009 indictment that prosecutors in New York used to charge Mr. Guzmán. Both Mr. Zambada's son, Vicente Zambada-Niebla, and his brother, Jesus Reynaldo Zambada García, are in custody in the United States and may appear as witnesses at the trial.

Jeffrey Lichtman, a defense lawyer for Joaquín Guzmán Loera, arriving at the federal courthouse in Brooklyn.

Mr. Calderón and Mr. Peña Nieto, the former Mexican presidents, put out statements on Twitter saying Mr. Lichtman's claims were "absolutely false."

Almost immediately after the defense offered its conspiracy theory, Judge Brian M. Cogan excused the jury for the day. In their absence, the judge cautioned Mr. Lichtman against making statements that might not be supported by evidence or that the judge's own rulings could preclude as inadmissible. Judge Cogan ordered both the defense and prosecution to submit written briefings on the claims, indicating that the main thrust of Mr. Guzmán's defense will now face judicial scrutiny even though the trial is underway.

In the nearly two years that Mr. Guzmán, 59, has been in custody in New York preparing for his long-awaited trial, his legal team has only given hints at a defense, sometimes suggesting at hearings and in court papers that he never played as central a role in the Sinaloa drug cartel as the government has claimed.

But Mr. Lichtman's speech on Tuesday posited what amounted to a complex, cross-border scheme to railroad Mr. Guzmán, one that was undertaken, he claimed, not only by compromised Mexican officials, but also by "crooked" agents of the Drug Enforcement Administration. The government's own witnesses will soon testify that some of those agents allowed Mr. Zambada to traffic drugs freely, Mr. Lichtman said.

The defense's arguments, which will continue Wednesday morning, came after Adam Fels, a federal prosecutor, told the jury the evidence would prove Mr. Guzmán was not only the cartel's leader, but the world's biggest drug dealer. Mr. Fels said that authorities in the United States have seized more than 40 tons of Mr. Guzmán's cocaine. That was enough, he said, to form 328 million separate lines of the drug.

Mr. Fels also said that during his long career, Mr. Guzmán had a payroll of corrupt officials and a violent army of sicarios — professional assassins — to protect his multibillion-dollar empire.

"Money, drugs, murder, a vast global narcotics trafficking organization," Mr. Fels told the jury. "That is what this case is about."

The government has accused Mr. Guzmán not only of having a hand in dozens of killings in his homeland, but also of running a sprawling organization that smuggled at least 200 tons of cocaine into the United States in a fleet of yachts, planes, fishing boats and submarines. Guzmán was convicted on drug and murder charges in Mexico in 1993, but escaped from prison twice — once, according to some accounts, in a jailhouse laundry cart and later on a motorcycle his associates left for him in a mile-long tunnel they dug into the shower of his cell.

Federal prosecutors plan to present a parade of cooperating witnesses and a mountain of evidence, including drug ledgers, satellite photos and secretly recorded audiotapes. They have promised that evidence will show that Mr. Guzmán raked in $14 billion in illicit profits.

The trial has received extraordinary media attention. So many journalists from the United States and Mexico showed up to cover the trial on Tuesday that the main courtroom and an auxiliary overflow room were filled within an hour. Dozens of reporters were stranded in a hallway unable to watch the proceeding at all.

Yet despite the anticipation, the trial began with a false start, Judge Cogan announcing that two of the 18 anonymous jurors needed to be dismissed.

One of them, Judge Cogan said, was "anxious and upset" at the prospect of sitting in judgment of Mr. Guzmán, a man said to be the most notorious and feared criminal of the 21st century. The other had complained that he would suffer financial hardship from being out of work during the four-month trial. The parties broke away for an emergency jury selection session, picking two new panelists by midafternoon.

Mr. Fels described the defendant as a seasoned trafficker who had ascended to the top of his cartel after getting a start growing poppies and marijuana in Sinaloa. He later made a name for himself as a speedy smuggler who worked with Colombian cartels.

But Mr. Lichtman said Mr. Guzmán was "a nobody" with "a second-grade education" who had for years been blamed for Mr. Zambada's wrongdoing. "There is another side to this story," he told the jury.

El Chapo Puts the Drug War on Trial

OPINION | BY IOAN GRILLO | NOV. 15, 2018

Joaquín Guzmán's prosecution will inadvertently highlight the government's failure to stop the flow of narcotics and the related bloodshed.

MEXICO CITY — An iconic photo from 1993 shows Colombian police officers smiling as they crouch over the bullet-ridden corpse of Pablo Escobar, who Forbes magazine had claimed was the richest drug trafficker on the planet. The picture was taken by Steve Murphy, an agent for the Drug Enforcement Administration, who helped track down the kingpin accused of fomenting mass murder in his homeland. Mr. Escobar's "fate should serve as an example to others who traffic in death and misery," said the drug czar Lee Brown, amid celebrations in Bogotá and Washington.

Fast forward 25 years, and a new supervillain, Joaquín Guzmán Loera, known as El Chapo, sits in a federal court in Brooklyn, accused of trafficking enough heroin, cocaine, marijuana and crystal meth to Americans to have made $14 billion over two and a half decades. Mr. Guzmán's infamy, including escaping from two maximum-security prisons in Mexico, puts him alongside Mr. Escobar and indeed the bootlegger Al Capone as the most notorious traffickers of modern times.

In the years between Mr. Escobar's death and Mr. Guzmán's trial, which began this week, the war on drugs has stumbled on. In terms of taking down kingpins and burning heaps of their narcotics, it has been a stunning success. It terms of reducing the number of Americans killed from overdoses or Latin Americans murdered over smuggling profits, it has been a resounding failure.

The Drug Policy Alliance estimates the fight against the illegal drug trade costs United States taxpayers $58 billion a year. But 2017 claimed a record 15,900 heroin overdose deaths, as well as highs in fatalities from cocaine, meth and fentanyl. In Mexico, the many-sided battle between rival drug cartels and an array of security forces is estimated to have killed more than 119,000 people over a decade. That's comparable to some of the worst continuing armed conflicts around the world and has destabilized swaths of the country. Most drug lords who are extradited to the United States cut deals. But Mr. Guzmán pleaded not guilty, forcing prosecutors to put together a case scheduled to last months. They say they will call witnesses, including his fellow traffickers, to describe how he smuggled dope in ingenious ways — such as in cans of jalapeño chilies — bribed Mexican officials at every level and masterminded the brutal murder of his enemies.

Eduardo Balarezo, one of Mr. Guzmán's defense lawyers, told me that he will challenge the witnesses and draw attention to any deals they may have made for their testimony, and that he will question the tactics of D.E.A. agents. In the past, agents have been criticized for the use of dubious informants and embedding with drug traffickers.

The prosecutors may well prove that Mr. Guzmán is guilty of heinous crimes. But they're also likely to inadvertently highlight the decades of failure to stop either the flow of drugs or the bloodshed, as well as particular D.E.A. tactics and the aid to Mexican security forces that suffer from corruption. As the world watches, it will be difficult not to wonder whether Mr. Guzmán's case is actually putting the war on drugs on trial.

That is not to say that Mr. Guzmán does not deserve to spend his life in prison if the jury finds him guilty. Covering cartel violence in Mexico since 2001, I have stared at hundreds of bloody corpses and heard the anguish of too many of their loved ones, which brings home the immense human cost. And D.E.A. agents risk their lives trying to stop this menace.

But even if Mr. Guzmán is sentenced to a maximum-security prison, it will not save families on both sides of the border from more drug overdoses and more drug violence. The victims deserve more.

Working out a better drug policy is a tough challenge, but we have a historic opportunity. Just a decade ago, many observers said that any drug legalization was a nonstarter. But on Nov. 6, Michigan became the 10th state to legalize recreational marijuana; Canada has legalized it and Mexico is taking steps in that direction.

We may never want shops openly selling heroin. But in addition to legalization of less dangerous drugs, a better effort could be made to get more addicts into rehab; a 2015 study found that almost 80 percent of Americans with problematic opioid use were not getting treatment. Methadone programs can also help some addicts and stop them from funding mass murder south of the Rio Grande.

A first step is simply to acknowledge that the current drug policy is failing. If it continues stumbling on, in another 25 years we'll probably be focused on a new kingpin, along with more tales of drug money, police corruption and mountains of corpses.

IOAN GRILLO is the author of "Gangster Warlords: Drug Dollars, Killing Fields, and the New Politics of Latin America" and a contributing opinion writer.

How El Chapo Became a Kingpin, According to a Witness

BY ALAN FEUER | NOV. 26, 2018

THE SMALL PLANE, filled with a ton of Colombian cocaine, ran out of fuel as it approached the secret airstrip near Agua Prieta, Mexico. Directed by a Mexican guide, the pilot landed the craft but couldn't slow it down. Both of its engines had died.

As the plane came skidding to a halt, the wheels snapped off, the guide told jurors on Monday.

And the million-dollar cargo?

"It was saved," he said.

That harrowing, but ultimately successful, flight was Miguel Angel Martínez's first full mission as an employee for a newcomer in the drug trade, a young ambitious trafficker named Joaquín Guzmán Loera. Well before he earned a billion-dollar fortune and was known to the world as El Chapo, Mr. Guzmán was the leader of a scrappy narcotics start-up, shipping drugs for Colombia's more powerful cartels and earning profits at a less-than-even split.

In his first day as a witness at Mr. Guzmán's drug conspiracy trial in Federal District Court in Brooklyn, Mr. Martínez described the early days of his former boss's career, providing something like a portrait of the kingpin as a young man.

Prosecutors are using Mr. Martínez to tell what amounts to Mr. Guzmán's origin story. Given his long friendship with the defendant, prosecutors have gone to great lengths to protect him.

Mr. Martínez testified on Monday that he was a founding member of Mr. Guzmán's initial crew, taking a job with him in 1987 as a pilot and later running his Mexico City administrative office.

Though it eventually employed hundreds of people, Mr. Guzmán's operation had only about 25 people in the late 1980s when it was just beginning, Mr. Martínez said. In those early days, the budding crime lord was cutting deals with Colombian suppliers as part of a larger organization, the Guadalajara drug cartel. Among those on his payroll were two of his cousins, Hector and Arturo Beltrán Leyva, who moved product north across the border to Los Angeles. A lawyer who was largely responsible for bribing the police was also part of the crew.

Mr. Martínez, who started as a pilot, soon became a kind of air traffic controller, scheduling and tracking dozens of flights carrying drug shipments from Colombia to a network of Mr. Guzmán's hidden airstrips.

He testified that he communicated by code with the pilots: fuel was "wine," he said, and the planes were referred to as "girls." To avoid police detection, he added, he would whistle to the pilots to let them know when it was safe to take off.

Mr. Martínez's success in taking Colombian cocaine safely into Mexico, he explained, endeared him to Mr. Guzmán, who soon became his son's godfather. The two men also started traveling together, Mr. Martínez recalled: once to Los Angeles, where Mr. Guzmán spent $6 million buying airplanes, and then to Las Vegas, where they gambled.

Mr. Guzmán also opened up to him, Mr. Martínez said, telling him how he got his start in dealing drugs by cultivating marijuana near his home in Sinaloa, Mexico, and making heroin by scraping — "little by little every morning" — the milk-like sap out of the poppies he had planted.

"He was a very poor person who didn't have anything to eat," Mr. Martínez said. "And that was the reason why he got involved in drug trafficking."

But Mr. Guzmán did not stay poor for long. In a bit of back story that was part of Mr. Martínez's testimony in a trial in 2006, he said Mr. Guzmán owned at least three Lear jets and moved about with an entourage of gunmen, shuttling among multiple homes in multiple Mexican cities. In one of those homes, there was a hidden compartment underneath a bed that raised off the floor on a hydraulic-powered lift. Mr. Guzmán also had a zoo in Guadalajara, Mr. Martínez noted in 2006, where he kept lions, tigers, crocodiles and bears.

Some of El Chapo's fortune was used to buy off the authorities, Mr. Martínez told the jury on Monday, including the chief of Mexico City's federal police. According to Mr. Martínez, Mr. Guzmán paid the police chief $10 million two or three times in the early 1990s. In exchange, he said, the chief gave the kingpin information about drug investigations and helped him track down his enemies and rivals.

At least twice since he was arrested by the Mexican authorities in 1998, assassins have tried to kill Mr. Martínez. The first attempt on his life came shortly after he was taken into custody. A group of killers confronted him in prison, stabbing him repeatedly. After a second knife attack, he testified at the separate trial in 2006, someone threw two hand grenades into his cell. He survived, he said, by hiding behind his toilet bowl.

Because of the threats he has faced, prosecutors in the case have taken several extraordinary measures, forbidding artists at the trial from sketching any portion of his face. The prosecutors even won permission from Judge Brian M. Cogan to check and evaluate the sketches before they were removed from the courtroom.

Despite these precautions, there was a small breach in security on Monday afternoon. Mr. Guzmán's wife, Emma Coronel Aispuro, somehow — against the rules — sneaked a cellphone into the courthouse just before Mr. Martínez took the stand. Ms. Coronel, a former beauty queen, has attended the trial each day since it began two weeks ago, and this was the first time she had caused any trouble.

Judge Cogan had a simple a solution to the problem. He ordered her to relinquish her phone and pass through the metal detectors again.

El Chapo's Early Days as a Budding Kingpin

BY ALAN FEUER AND EMILY PALMER | DEC. 2, 2018

THE JURORS AT THE TRIAL of Joaquín Guzmán Loera, known as El Chapo, were treated last week to a cinematic narrative about the early years of the kingpin's career, detailing his rise from a young upstart in the drug trade to a wealthy and successful narco-entrepreneur.

Much of the tale was told by one of El Chapo's first employees, Miguel Angel Martínez, who began working for the cartel as a pilot in 1987 before being promoted to running operations in Mexico City.

Over four days last week as a government witness in Federal District Court in Brooklyn, Mr. Martínez described how the crime lord went from being a novice trafficker with a staff of only 25 people to earning hundreds of millions of dollars that he spent on extravagances like a fleet of private jets and a rural ranch with a zoo where guests could ride a train past crocodiles and bears.

But as with many drug-world relationships, the bond between the two men ultimately soured. In this case, that occurred in 1998, after Mr. Martínez was arrested.

The kingpin trusted Mr. Martínez so completely that he placed many of his real-estate holdings in his name, including a house where one of his mistresses was living. Mr. Martínez, in custody and facing mounting legal fees, sold the home without permission.

Within months, a team of assassins confronted him in jail, stabbing him seven times, he said. He survived, but suffered another knife attack, he told the jury last week, before the authorities moved him to a different jail. Even there, however, he faced death threats.

One night as he slept in his cell, he recalled, he was awakened by a band outside that was playing one of Mr. Guzmán's favorite songs, Un Puño de Tierra. Mr. Martínez considered it a message from Mr. Guzmán.

Security at the Federal District Court in Brooklyn was tighter than usual in anticipation of Miguel Angel Martínez's testimony.

Early the next morning, an assassin appeared outside his cell. This would-be killer, he said, pointed a pistol at the jail guard's head and demanded that he open the door. When the guard said that he didn't have a key, the assassin tossed two hand grenades at the cell door. Mr. Martínez told the jury that he survived the explosions by shielding himself in the bathroom.

EARLY DAYS AS A SMUGGLER

On Thursday, after Mr. Martínez was excused, the jury got a glimpse into Mr. Guzmán's skills as a smuggler from his chief cocaine supplier, the Colombian drug lord Juan Carlos Ramírez Abadía.

A leader of the North Valley drug cartel, Mr. Ramírez recalled how in 1990 Mr. Guzmán moved their first shared load of cocaine through Mexico to Los Angeles in less than a week — much faster, he noted, than the month it took most other Mexican traffickers.

He seemed especially impressed by Mr. Guzmán's secret airstrip where his five planes landed after arriving from Colombia. The strip was not only well lighted, Mr. Ramírez said, but the Mexican ground crew also refueled planes quickly. The pilots were even given an early morning meal.

A team of Mexican federal police officers protected, and often took part in, the unloading of drugs, Mr. Ramírez said.

Known as Chupeta — slang for "lollipop" — Mr. Ramírez was one of the most astonishing figures to testify so far. Before his arrest in Brazil in 2007, he surgically altered his entire face — cheekbones, jaw, eyes, mouth, nose and ears — to avoid detection by the authorities. On the witness stand he looked like a character out of an old Dick Tracy comic. He testified, without explanation, in a pair of gloves and a zipped-up winter parka.

Mr. Ramírez is scheduled to return to court on Monday. According to court papers filed over the weekend, he will likely testify about coded ledgers in which he recorded his drug deals with El Chapo.

FIND THE PERFECT ARCHITECT

Mr. Guzmán is widely known for building tunnels that he used to quickly export cocaine from Mexico to the United States. But the man who deserves much of the early credit for those tunnels is Felipe Corona, who devised a tunnel from Agua Prieta to Douglas, Ariz., that allowed Mr. Guzmán to bring cocaine into the United States in less than 24 hours.

Mr. Corona also built bodegas and homes with "clavos," or hidden compartments, to stash drugs and money.

In these homes, the main bedrooms contained switches hidden in the windows. By pressing the switch, the bed frame and floor would lift up to reveal a secure room with steps, a ladder and a "very big, very secure safe," Mr. Martínez testified.

Mr. Martínez, who met Mr. Corona at Mr. Guzmán's house in 1987, saw some of these structures first hand and even lived in one of the houses.

Another such clavo, which he described as being underwater, included a cistern. Draining the water would reveal a ladder, which would be used to gain access into a special compartment.

LESSONS IN MONEY LAUNDERING

On the stand, Mr. Martínez detailed how a cartel launders money:

• Use small bills, mostly $20s.

• Use "straw parties" (typically people who give up their ID for money so that drug money can be hidden in their name) or "front companies" (legitimate businesses that also deal in drugs in the background).

• Ignorance is bliss. Typically, most members of the cartel don't know where the money is hidden in order to avoid seizure if anyone is caught.

• Infiltrate "casas del cambio," or money exchanges, which work with banks. Traffickers can get prepaid cards (with hundreds of dollars on it) which are easier to pack than cash.

COCAINE LOST AT SEA

In the early 1990s one 10-ton shipment of cocaine, worth approximately $178 million, was lost at sea when the cartel tried to transport it during a hurricane, Mr. Martínez told jurors.

Mr. Guzmán deployed all four of his jets to look for the shipment but "we never heard from it again," Mr. Martínez said. "Not the boat, or the crew or the drugs."

El Chapo Trial: Why His I.T. Guy Had a Nervous Breakdown

BY ALAN FEUER | JAN. 10, 2019

NOT LONG AFTER his 21st birthday, Christian Rodriguez got the contract of a lifetime for his new info-tech company: The Colombian was hired as a cybersecurity consultant by Joaquín Guzmán Loera, the Mexican drug lord known as El Chapo.

While Mr. Rodriguez had little experience or formal education, he had been recommended by one of his other clients: Jorge Cifuentes Villa, a veteran trafficker who worked with Mr. Guzmán making cocaine deals with left-wing guerrillas in Colombia.

And so in 2008, the ambitious, young techie visited Mr. Guzmán at one of his hide-outs deep in the Sierra Madre mountains, inspecting the kingpin's communications system and his shoddy internet setup, which often broke down when it rained. In several follow-up meetings, Mr. Rodriguez testified this week, he pitched Mr. Guzmán on an elaborate plan to enhance his information security, offering to build him a private phone network that ran on the internet and was totally encrypted.

That sophisticated system was, within three years, used against Mr. Guzmán after Mr. Rodriguez became ensnared in an F.B.I. sting operation and was then persuaded to become an informant. The I.T. expert helped the American authorities secretly collect a vast trove of the kingpin's phone calls and text messages — among them, dozens he had sent to his wife and mistresses. In two days of testimony that ended on Thursday, Mr. Rodriguez told this riveting story to great — and damaging — effect at Mr. Guzmán's drug conspiracy trial in Federal District Court in Brooklyn.

Mr. Rodriguez's account was a kind of 21st-century cautionary tale. The moral? Always treat your I.T. people well. It was also a high-tech spy thriller in which federal agents were able to leverage Mr. Guzmán's obsession with espionage against him.

It all began when Mr. Rodriguez, now 32, took $100,000 to build the kingpin the encrypted network, which allowed as many as 100 members of the Sinaloa drug cartel to speak securely with each other merely by dialing three-digit extensions on their phones. Part of his contract, Mr. Rodriguez said, was to teach the kingpin's team how to use the phones, recalling that he once gave a tutorial on the devices to Mr. Guzmán's personal secretary in an armored car.

But Mr. Guzmán — who, according to witnesses, long had a penchant for snooping — wanted something more. The I.T. expert said the crime lord also asked him to install spyware called FlexiSPY on the "special phones" he had given to his wife, Emma Coronel Aispuro, as well as to two of his lovers, including one who was a former Mexican lawmaker.

The kingpin made other strange requests, Mr. Rodriguez told jurors on Thursday. Once, he said, Mr. Guzmán asked him to find a way to intercept every message being sent from every internet cafe in Culiacán, a city of about 800,000 residents in the crime lord's home state of Sinaloa. (Mr. Rodriguez said he tried, but ultimately failed.)

Working for a narco-lord could also be dangerous, he said.

Not long after the assignment to tap the internet cafes, the Mexican military raided Mr. Guzmán's secret mountain hide-out. Mr. Rodriguez said he was forced to wander for three days in the elevated terrain with the kingpin and a band of heavily armed bodyguards. The gunmen, Mr. Rodriguez recalled, carried both "large weapons" and one "very large weapon," which, they told him, was capable of shooting down a helicopter.

Throughout the grueling journey, Mr. Guzmán was "always very calm, very sure, very tranquil," Mr. Rodriguez said.

When a prosecutor asked the young techie how he felt being on the lam, he answered, "very badly."

After that experience, Mr. Rodriguez said he decided to put some "distance" between himself and Mr. Guzmán's organization, training other technicians to run the cartel's day-to-day communications.

Shortly after, he recounted, the F.B.I. launched a covert operation to secure his cooperation.

In February 2010, an F.B.I. agent testified Tuesday, an undercover officer posing as a Russian mobster met Mr. Rodriguez in a Manhattan hotel. The officer said he wanted the I.T. expert to devise a way for him to speak with his associates without law enforcement listening in.

The following year, Mr. Rodriguez said on Thursday, two other federal agents approached him in Bogotá, Colombia, saying they knew he worked for Mr. Guzmán and telling him he was "in serious trouble."

That same day, Mr. Rodriguez said, he agreed to become a government informant. Over the next several months, he said he installed recording software in Mr. Guzmán's network that automatically sent copies of the kingpin's calls to the F.B.I. each day at midnight. Mr. Rodriguez also gave the bureau the user names and passwords of Mr. Guzmán's FlexiSPY accounts, allowing agents to read — almost in real time — the intimate and incriminating texts he sent his romantic partners.

All this came crashing down in 2012 when Mr. Rodriguez intercepted a phone call between two of Jorge Cifuentes's siblings in which he heard them saying they had figured out that El Chapo's tech guy was working with the Americans. After fleeing to the United States, Mr. Rodriguez said he had a "nervous breakdown" within a year. He was hospitalized and treated with electroconvulsive therapy.

This week, he looked better, if not completely fine, telling jurors he was now on medication and seeing a psychiatrist.

As he finished his testimony, Mr. Rodriguez left the witness stand and walked out the courtroom door, nervously avoiding Mr. Guzmán's gaze.

El Chapo Found Guilty on
All Counts; Faces Life in Prison

BY ALAN FEUER | FEB. 12, 2019

THE MEXICAN CRIME LORD known as El Chapo was convicted on Tuesday after a three-month drug trial in New York that exposed the inner workings of his sprawling cartel, which over decades shipped tons of drugs into the United States and plagued Mexico with relentless bloodshed and corruption.

The guilty verdict against the kingpin, whose real name is Joaquín Guzmán Loera, ended the career of a legendary outlaw who also served as a dark folk hero in Mexico, notorious for his innovative smuggling tactics, his violence against competitors, his storied prison breaks and his nearly unstoppable ability to evade the Mexican authorities.

As Judge Brian M. Cogan read the jury's charge sheet in open court — 10 straight guilty verdicts on all 10 counts of the indictment — Mr. Guzmán sat listening to a translator, looking stunned. When the reading of the verdict was complete, Mr. Guzmán leaned back to glance at his wife, Emma Coronel Aispuro, who flashed him a thumbs up with tears in her eyes.

The jury's decision came more than a week after the panel started deliberations at the trial in Federal District Court in Brooklyn where prosecutors presented a mountain of evidence against the cartel leader, including testimony from 56 witnesses, 14 of whom once worked with Mr. Guzmán.

Mr. Guzmán now faces life in prison at his sentencing hearing, scheduled for June 25.

Speaking to reporters outside the courthouse, Richard P. Donoghue, the United States attorney for the Eastern District of New York, called the guilty verdict a victory for law enforcement; for Mexico, where 100,000 people had died because of drug violence; and for families who had lost someone to the "black hole of addiction."

"There are those who say the war on drugs is not worth fighting," Mr. Donoghue added. "Those people are wrong."

In their own news conference, Mr. Guzmán's lawyers promised an appeal, saying they would focus on the extradition process that brought the kingpin to Brooklyn for trial and on the prosecution's efforts to restrict their cross-examinations of witnesses. They said that Mr. Guzmán had expected the guilty verdict and was prepared for it.

"I've never faced a case with so many cooperating witnesses and so much evidence," Jeffrey Lichtman, one of Mr. Guzmán's lawyers, said. "We did all we could as defense lawyers."

A. Eduardo Balarezo, another one of Mr. Guzmán's lawyers, added about his client: "When he came here he was already presumed guilty by everyone, unfortunately. We weren't just fighting evidence, we were fighting perception."

Not long after the jury got the case on Feb. 4, Matthew G. Whitaker, the acting United States attorney general, stepped into the courtroom and shook hands with each of the trial prosecutors, wishing them good luck. Over the next several days, the jurors, appearing to scrutinize the government's evidence, asked to be given thousands of pages of testimony, including — in an unusual move — the full testimonies of six different prosecution witnesses.

Mr. Guzmán's trial, which took place under intense media scrutiny and tight security from bomb-sniffing dogs, police snipers and federal marshals with radiation sensors, was the first time an American jury heard details about the financing, logistics and bloody history of one of the drug cartels that have long pumped huge amounts of heroin, cocaine, marijuana and synthetic drugs like fentanyl into the United States, earning traffickers billions of dollars.

But despite extensive testimony about private jets filled with cash, bodies burned in bonfires and shocking evidence that Mr. Guzmán and his men often drugged and raped young girls, the case also revealed the operatic, even absurd, nature of cartel culture. It featured accounts of traffickers taking target practice with a bazooka, a mariachi playing all night outside a jail cell and a murder plot involving a cyanide-laced arepa.

At times, the trial was so bizarre it felt like a drug-world telenovela unfolding live in the courtroom. Last month, one of Mr. Guzmán's mistresses tearfully proclaimed her love for him even as she testified against him. The following day, in what seemed like a coordinated show of solidarity, the kingpin and his wife, Emma Coronel Aispuro, appeared in court in matching red velvet smoking jackets.

Toward the end of the proceeding, Alejandro Edda, an actor who plays El Chapo on the Netflix series "Narcos: Mexico," showed up at the trial to study Mr. Guzmán. The crime lord flashed an ecstatic smile when told Mr. Edda had come to see him.

Although Tuesday's conviction dealt a blow to the Sinaloa drug cartel, which Mr. Guzmán, 61, helped to run for decades, the group continues to operate, led in part by the kingpin's sons. In 2016 and 2017, the years when Mr. Guzmán was arrested for a final time and sent for prosecution to New York, Mexican heroin production increased by 37 percent and fentanyl seizures at the southwest border more than doubled, according to the Drug Enforcement Administration.

The D.E.A., in its most recent assessment of the drug trade, noted that Mr. Guzmán's organization and a rising power, the Jalisco New Generation cartel, "remain the greatest criminal drug threat" to the United States.

The Mexican authorities began pursuing the stocky crime lord — whose nickname translates roughly to "Shorty" — in 1993 when he was blamed for a killing that epitomized for many Mexicans the extreme violence of the country's drug wars: the assassination of the Roman Catholic cardinal Juan Jesús Posadas Ocampo at the Guadalajara airport.

Though Mr. Guzmán was convicted that same year on charges of murdering the cardinal, he escaped from prison in 2001 — in a laundry cart pushed by a jailhouse janitor — and spent the next decade either on the lam in one of his mountain hide-outs or slipping through various police and military dragnets.

Emma Coronel Aispuro, the wife of Joaquín Guzmán Loera, known as El Chapo, was surrounded by media after the verdict on Tuesday.

In 2012, he evaded capture by the F.B.I. and the Mexican federal police by ducking out the back door of his oceanview mansion in Los Cabos into a patch of thorn bushes. Two years later, after he was recaptured in a hotel in Mazatlán by the D.E.A. and the Mexican marines, he escaped from prison again — this time, through a lighted, ventilated, mile-long tunnel dug into the shower of his cell.

But following his last arrest — after a gunfight in Los Mochis, Mexico, in 2016 — Mr. Guzmán was extradited to Brooklyn, where federal prosecutors had initially indicted him in 2009. He also faced indictment in six other American judicial districts.

The top charge of the Brooklyn indictment named Mr. Guzmán as a principal leader of a "continuing criminal enterprise" to purchase drugs from suppliers in Colombia, Ecuador, Panama and Mexico's Golden Triangle — an area including the states of Sinaloa, Durango and Chihuahua where most of the country's heroin and marijuana are produced.

It also accused him of earning a jaw-dropping $14 billion during his career by smuggling up to 200 tons of drugs across the United States border in an array of yachts, speedboats, long-range fishing boats, airplanes, cargo trains, semi-submersible submarines, tractor-trailers filled with frozen meat and cans of jalapeños and yet another tunnel (hidden under a pool table in Agua Prieta, Mexico).

The prosecution was years in the making and Mr. Guzmán's trial drew upon investigative work by the F.B.I., the D.E.A., the United States Coast Guard, Homeland Security Investigations and federal prosecutors in Chicago, Miami, San Diego, Washington, New York and El Paso. The trial team also relied on scores of local American police officers and the authorities in Ecuador, Colombia and the Dominican Republic.

The evidence presented at the trial included dozens of surveillance photos, three sets of detailed drug ledgers, several of the defendant's handwritten letters and hundreds of his most intimate — and incriminating — phone calls and text messages intercepted through four separate wiretap operations.

Prosecutors used all of this to trace Mr. Guzmán's 30-year rise from a young, ambitious trafficker with a knack for speedy smuggling to a billionaire narco lord with an entourage of maids and secretaries, a portfolio of vacation homes — even a ranch with a personal zoo.

Andrea Goldbarg, an assistant United States attorney, called the prosecution's case "an avalanche" during the government's summations. Even with the help of a PowerPoint presentation, complete with a slide show of photos of the kingpin, Ms. Goldbarg took almost an entire day to lead the jury through it.

But the centerpiece of the government's offering was testimony from a Shakespearean cast of cooperating witnesses who took the stand to spill the deepest secrets of Mr. Guzmán's personal and professional lives.

Among the witnesses were the kingpin's first employee; one of his personal secretaries; his chief Colombian cocaine supplier; the son of his closest partner and heir apparent to his empire; his I.T.

expert; his top American distributor; a killer in his army of assassins; even the young mistress with whom he escaped from the Mexican marines, naked, through a tunnel that was hidden under a bathtub in his safe house.

Confronting this onslaught, Mr. Guzmán's lawyers offered little in the way of an affirmative defense, opting instead to use cross-examination to attack the credibility of the witnesses, most of whom were seasoned criminals with their own long histories of lying, cheating, drug dealing and killing.

Late last month, there was frenzied speculation that Mr. Guzmán might testify in his own defense. But after he decided against doing so, the entire defense case lasted only 30 minutes — compared with 10 weeks for the prosecution — and consisted of a single witness and a stipulation read into the record.

In his closing argument, Mr. Lichtman, one of the defense lawyers, reprised a theme he first introduced during his opening statement in November, telling jurors that the real mastermind of the cartel was Mr. Guzmán's closest partner, Ismael Zambada García.

Despite being sought by the police in Mexico for nearly 50 years, Mr. Zambada, known as El Mayo, has never been arrested. Mr. Lichtman said the reason was that Mr. Zambada had bribed virtually the entire Mexican government. Mr. Guzmán was merely "the rabbit" that the authorities chased for decades, deflecting attention from his partner, Mr. Lichtman said.

Witness after witness took the stand at the trial and talked about paying off nearly every level of the Mexican police, military and political establishment — including the shocking allegation that Mr. Guzmán gave a $100 million bribe to the country's former president, Enrique Peña Nieto, in the run-up to Mexico's 2012 elections.

There was also testimony that bribes were paid to Genaro García Luna, one of Mexico's top former law enforcement officers, a host of Mexican generals and police officials, and almost the entire congress of Colombia.

"One of the important things about this conviction is that it sends a resounding message," Ángel Meléndez, special agent in charge for Homeland Security Investigations, said of other drug traffickers. "You're not unreachable, you're not untouchable and your day will come."

EMILY PALMER contributed reporting.

'El Chapo' Guzmán Sentenced to Life in Prison, Ending Notorious Criminal Career

BY ALAN FEUER | JULY 17, 2019

He sent hundreds of tons of drugs to the United States from Mexico and caused the brutal deaths of dozens of people.

HE WAS ONE of the most notorious outlaws of the last 100 years: a brutal Mexican cartel leader, a wily trafficker who smuggled more than $12 billion worth of drugs and plunged his country into a long-running tragedy of bloodshed and corruption.

But on Wednesday morning, the 30-year criminal career of Joaquín Guzmán Loera, known to the world as El Chapo, reached its final chapter as a federal judge in New York City sentenced him to life in prison.

The life term, mandated by law as a result of the severity of Mr. Guzmán's crimes, was handed down in Federal District Court in Brooklyn, where the kingpin was convicted last winter of drug, murder and money laundering charges after a sprawling three-month trial.

As some of the federal agents who had chased him for years looked on from the gallery, Judge Brian M. Cogan issued the sentence and Mr. Guzmán, 62, was hauled away to prepare himself — pending an appeal — for spending the rest of his life behind bars.

Before he disappeared into a holding cell behind the courtroom, he blew a kiss to his wife, Emma Coronel Aispuro, who attended most of his trial and was implicated in a handful of his crimes.

Although Judge Cogan had no choice but to sentence Mr. Guzmán to life, he noted that the "overwhelming evil" of the drug lord's crimes was readily apparent. Beyond the life sentence — plus an additional 30 years — he ordered him to pay a staggering $12.6 billion in forfeiture.

Looking disheveled and slightly out of sorts, Mr. Guzmán walked into the eighth-floor courtroom under guard shortly before 9:30 a.m.

He wore a loosefitting gray suit, with his tie rakishly askew and a new-growth mustache darkening his upper lip.

Reading from a prepared statement, he said he had not received a fair trial and complained about his solitary confinement in Manhattan's federal jail, calling it "psychological, emotional and mental torture 24 hours a day."

"Since the government of the United States is going to send me to a prison where my name will never be heard again, I take advantage of this opportunity to say there was no justice here," he said.

Though Judge Cogan did not specify where Mr. Guzmán would serve his sentence, he is likely to be sent to the country's most forbidding federal prison, the United States Penitentiary Administrative Maximum Facility, or ADX, in Florence, Colo.

Mr. Guzmán's decades-long career atop the Sinaloa drug cartel, one of Mexico's most powerful criminal mafias, came to a close only after years of joint investigation and pursuit by the American and Mexican authorities.

His ability to persistently evade capture — and then escape from prison after he was caught — underscored the deep corruption of the Mexican government by his cartel, which used bribery and intimidation to control not just the local, state and federal police, but some of the highest-ranking officials in the national government.

"It's justice not only for the Mexican government, but for all of Guzmán's victims in Mexico," said Raymond P. Donovan, the agent in charge of the New York office of the Drug Enforcement Administration, who was instrumental in capturing the kingpin twice.

After the sentencing, one of Mr. Guzmán's lawyers, Jeffrey Lichtman, spoke outside the courthouse in the Brooklyn Heights neighborhood, complaining, as his client had, that the lengthy legal proceeding had been unfair.

"All he wanted was justice and at the end of the day, he didn't get it," Mr. Lichtman said, adding, "It was a show trial, and it's been so since Day 1."

Moments later, Richard P. Donoghue, the United States attorney in Brooklyn, whose office prosecuted the case with colleagues from Miami and Washington, also addressed reporters.

Mr. Donoghue said the authorities could not undo the misery Mr. Guzmán had caused, "but we can ensure that he spends every minute of every day of the rest of his life in prison."

The trial took place under intense media scrutiny and tight security that involved bomb-sniffing dogs, police snipers and federal marshals with radiation sensors. The verdict on Feb. 12 came after more than a week of deliberations by the jury. Ultimately, Mr. Guzmán was found guilty on all 10 counts of the indictment.

Prosecutors leveled some of the most serious charges possible against him, presenting evidence that he sent hundreds of tons of drugs to the United States from Mexico and caused the deaths of dozens of people to protect himself and his smuggling routes.

The case revealed in exacting detail the inner workings of the Sinaloa drug cartel, such as how it employed I.T. consultants and how it packaged its cocaine in rubber "condoms."

But given the defendant's fame and notoriety, the trial was also a boisterous legal circus, complete with a horde of international reporters, a steady trickle of curious "narco-tourists" and a cameo appearance by an actor who plays the drug lord on a Netflix show.

The American authorities began their hunt for the kingpin as far back as the early 1990s, when he was indicted on separate federal charges in Tucson and San Diego.

The two indictments were filed just before and somewhat after he was arrested while on the run in Guatemala and then returned to Mexico, where he was tried and imprisoned for the 1993 murder of Juan Jesús Posadas Ocampo, a beloved Roman Catholic cardinal.

In 2001, however, Mr. Guzmán broke out of prison — by many accounts, in the bottom of a laundry cart — and spent the next 13 years playing cat-and-mouse with the law.

He evaded both arrest and the five subsequent indictments filed against him in the United States, largely by shuttling among a series of hide-outs in the Sierra Madre mountains in the Mexican state of Sinaloa.

In February 2012, the Mexican and American authorities came within inches of nabbing him in an ocean-view mansion in Cabo San Lucas, Mexico.

But he was not caught until Mr. Donovan and a coalition of law enforcement and military officers on both sides of the border mounted a wiretap operation that cracked Mr. Guzmán's communications network. He was found in a beachfront condominium in Mazatlán, Mexico, in February 2014.

Within a year and a half, however, he had escaped again — this time, through a sophisticated tunnel that opened into the shower of his prison cell. A coalition similar to the one that caught him in 2014 redoubled its efforts and captured the kingpin for a second time, after a violent gunfight, in Los Mochis, Mexico, in early 2016.

When Mr. Guzmán finally stood trial in New York in November, his conviction was all but assured given the mountains of evidence collected against him over the years.

Some of that evidence came from incriminating intercepts from the various wiretaps over which agents had for months been listening in on the kingpin and his underlings. But just as damaging were the 14 witnesses from inside his cartel — suppliers, distributors, top lieutenants, even one of his mistresses — who testified against him.

Since his extradition to the United States in January 2017, Mr. Guzmán has been held in 10 South, the maximum-security wing of the Manhattan federal jail. On Wednesday, he told Judge Cogan that since arriving there he had been forced to drink "unsanitary water" and wear earplugs made from toilet paper to drown out the racket of the ventilation system.

In response, Gina Parlovecchio, a federal prosecutor, said it was ironic that Mr. Guzmán had complained about undignified treatment in jail given that he showed no respect to his countless victims, not just those he killed or hunted, but the thousands who were harmed by the drugs he "pumped onto the streets," earning him a vast fortune of "blood money."

One of those victims, Andrea Velez, spoke out in court on Wednesday. She described through her tears how Mr. Guzmán had paid a Canadian chapter of the Hells Angels $1 million in a failed plot to murder her. Ms. Velez was at one point the personal assistant to one of the kingpin's top lieutenants, Alex Cifuentes Villa, but eventually became an F.B.I. informant who spied on the drug lord and his allies.

"I'm a miracle of God," Ms. Velez said, "because Mr. Guzmán tried to kill me."

EMILY PALMER contributed reporting.

CHAPTER 2

Latin America and the Drug Trade

From numerous revolutions, counter-revolutions and efforts by the United States to support regime change in Latin America, continuous instability in the region has fostered a haven for large-scale criminal enterprises. Chief among these has been the sale of narcotics. Latin America also has a fertile and diverse ecosystem that is well suited for growing crops for the production of illegal drugs. As a result of these factors, Latin America has become home to more drug kingpins than any other region in the world.

Latin Drug Cartels, Squeezed, Are Turning to Ecuador

BY RICHARD L. BERKE | MARCH 25, 1999

WASHINGTON, MARCH 24 — As other Latin American countries clamp down on illicit narcotics, Ecuador is emerging as an important shipment point both for importing chemicals needed to produce cocaine and for exporting the drug itself to the United States, Federal officials say.

Wedged between the two major cocaine exporting countries, Colombia to the north and Peru to the south, Ecuador has not traditionally been considered an important link in the international narcotics trade. And unlike its neighbors, it has not recently received significant increases in United States aid to battle drugs.

But authorities on drug trafficking and American intelligence reports indicate that as Colombia and Peru become more aggressive in fighting traffickers, the Colombian drug cartels are increasingly turning to Ecuador. Ecuador is a natural alternative because of its accessible seaports, good inland transportation routes, proximity to drug-producing countries and relatively loose drug laws.

'NEW TARGET OF OPPORTUNITY'

American officials have also expressed concern that Ecuador could become a money-laundering center because of its bank secrecy laws.

"It was always assumed that once we developed a new choke point there would be a means for a new port of entry," Senator Richard H. Bryan, a Nevada Democrat who has pushed for tighter export control of drug-related chemicals, said in an interview. "And Ecuador seems to be a new target of opportunity."

The Administration's concerns about Ecuador are underscored in a recent American intelligence report. "Record-setting seizures in Europe and the United States of cocaine shipments in Ecuadorean commercial vessels with origin in Ecuador establish beyond any doubt that Ecuador is an important transit country for illegal narcotics," the report said. "Ecuador is also a transit country for large quantities of precursor chemicals used to process cocaine in Colombia."

CHEMICAL IMPORTS ARE UP

Most chemicals that enter Ecuador are exported from the United States for legitimate industrial purposes. But front companies operated by traffickers often take control of the shipments so they can use the solvents, which are essential for refining cocaine into a usable form from coca leaves.

The United States receives the bulk of cocaine shipped from Ecuador, say officials from the Drug Enforcement Administration, State Department and Customs Service, who estimate that the volume is 30 to 50 metric tons a year and rising. Cocaine production worldwide is estimated at 776 metric tons a year.

The increase in chemicals smuggled through Ecuador for the processing of cocaine is more difficult to estimate, officials said. But Ecuadorean Government figures show that chemical imports into Ecuador increased by 29 percent in the first half of 1989 over the comparable period a year earlier.

John P. Walters, chief of staff to William J. Bennett, the national drug control policy director, said Ecuador was "the logical next target of the traffickers" and posed a greater threat than other countries in the region where traffickers are expected to turn, like Venezuela, Paraguay, Argentina, Chile and Brazil.

Mr. Walters praised Ecuador for being "very sensitive to attempts by Colombia traffickers to move in," and noted that the country has already succeeded in wiping out almost all of its coca cultivation.

BANKING CONTROLS ENACTED

Even so, it is not clear how committed Ecuador is to cracking down on smugglers. A spokesman for the Ecuadorean Embassy here, speaking on the condition that he not be identified, acknowledged that there was a growing problem, but he emphasized that the demand for cocaine was fueled by the United States.

"We don't have the problem of drug use," the spokesman said. "We don't have to deal with the problems of other countries."

Some steps have been taken by Ecuador, like the recent establishment of a Government panel there to investigate the source and destination of chemical imports. The Government has also enacted new controls on transferring bank shares to suspected traffickers and has proposed other measures to tighten restrictions on the drug trade.

Administration officials and intelligence reports say chemicals are imported to major ports in Ecuador. While some cocaine laboratories have been set up in Ecuador to process the chemicals, production there is negligible and the chemicals are usually smuggled to Colombia or Peru by land or sometimes by river routes.

Chemicals are easier to take into Ecuador, American authorities said, because unlike its neighbors, it has not imposed strict controls on the import of chemicals. These authorities also said that Ecuador, a country about the size of Colorado, lacks adequate automation to track the import of chemicals or the export of drugs.

The risk of prosecution in Ecuador is also lower than in nearby countries, American officials said, because Ecuadorean laws provide for prosecution only in cases where traffickers are actually caught possessing drugs. No laws allow tracking of assets, undercover operations or prosecutions for conspiracy.

Cali, the 'Quiet' Drug Cartel, Profits by Accommodation

BY JAMES BROOKE | JULY 14, 1991

CALI, COLOMBIA — Translating the slogan "Support your local police" into bricks and mortar, the leaders of Cali's cocaine cartel reportedly helped pay for the tidy police posts that dot this Colombian city's middle-class neighborhoods in a drive to suppress street crime.

In contrast, the capos of the rival Medellín cocaine cartel adopted a different policy toward their city's police force last year: a $4,000 bounty for each officer killed. By the time the offer was withdrawn, about 400 policemen in the Medellín area were dead.

This difference in style explains why Colombia's drug war has been almost exclusively directed at the Medellín cartel, based 250 miles north of here.

Indeed, after the surrender last month of Pablo Escobar Gaviria, chief of the Medellín cartel, there has been little sign that the authorities intend to tangle with the deeply entrenched Cali cartel, even though it has supplanted Medellín as the nation's No. 1 drug organization.

With friends all over, the Cali cartel poses a more daunting and insidious challenge to the Government of President Cesar Gaviria Trujillo.

"In Medellín, the cartel competed with the state," said Alvaro Guzmán, a sociologist here. "In Cali, there has been a process of accommodation with the state."

Over the last two years, Colombia's security forces have killed or jailed the Medellín organization's top leaders, extending special treatment to top bosses like Mr. Escobar who agree to give themselves up. The cartel's share of Colombia's $5 billion in annual cocaine exports has dropped from about 70 percent in mid-1989 to about 40 percent today.

Over the same period, Cali, the "quiet cartel," has expanded its market share from about 30 percent to about 60 percent, as it has been left largely untouched by the authorities.

"The tables have turned," Robert C. Bonner, head of the Drug Enforcement Administration, said from Washington. "There is no question that the Cali cartel is the predominant cocaine distribution organization in the world."

But given the trauma caused by the long war with the Medellín cartel, the Colombian Government apparently does not share Washington's view that the Cali drug traffickers should be confronted head-on, despite a pledge by President Gaviria to treat all cartels equally.

["We have the same policy toward the Cali cartel as toward the Medellín cartel," the President said in an interview Friday in Bogotá. "Simply because the Medellín cartel bore the greatest responsibility for narco-terrorism, we concentrated the largest amount of our efforts there. But our policy is the same."

[He said he hoped that Cali cartel members would take advantage of his plea-bargain policy to surrender for internment.]

AND WHAT OF THE CONSUMERS?

Many Colombians believe that Government strategy is to maintain sufficient pressure on drug traffickers to contain their activity in this country and induce them to move to neighboring Latin American countries.

Colombian officials maintain that since market forces sustain the cocaine trade, trafficking will end only when demand abates in the United States and Europe.

"The United States is putting on a lot of pressure over the Cali cartel," said Enrique Santos Calderon, a newspaper columnist. "But I don't think the Government is going to gratuitously start up a new 'narco-war.' "

Here in Colombia's third-largest city, the prevailing mood is one of discomfort over the international attention now focused on the local drug traffickers, who long ago wove themselves into Cali's society as seemingly upstanding white-collar citizens.

Few officials want to discuss what may be the city's largest business. The list of officials who declined interview requests included

A mug shot of Gilberto José Rodríguez Orejuela, one of the three leaders of the Cali cocaine cartel in Colombia.

the mayor, the state governor, the local prosecutor, and the city and state police chiefs.

In recent moves against the cartel, Colombia's Army destroyed 10 small cocaine-refining laboratories belonging to Cali traffickers.

MEN WITH PROTECTIVE SHIELDS

But Colombia still has not lodged charges against Gilberto Rodriguez Orejuela, reportedly the godfather of the Cali cartel, a loose confederation of about 15 groups.

"There may be a show of a few seizures around Cali, but the Government is not going to touch the leaders," a European envoy in Bogotá predicted.

The police here have denied collaborating with the Cali cartel. But Mr. Escobar of the Medellín group, from confinement, called Gilberto Rodriguez and his brother, Miguel, "pets of the police."

"The Rodriguez brothers dedicated themselves to informing on me and joined in association with" Colombia's top police officials, Mr. Escobar charged in an interview with a Medellín newspaper.

At stake for the two organizations is control of Colombia's most successful export commodity. According to a recent study by Salomon Kalmanovitz, a Bogotá economist, traffickers in 1990 brought back as much as $3.5 billion — roughly triple the amount earned from the sale of coffee, the country's largest legal export.

In recent years, while the Medellín cartel was thrown on the defensive, the Cali group moved out of its distribution base in New York into Miami and Los Angeles, markets previously dominated by Medellín. And using ports in the Netherlands and Spain it penetrated Europe, particularly Germany.

Unlike the Medellín cartel, which prefers fast shipment by plane and speedboat, the Cali traffickers hide their merchandise in freighter cargo containers. Cali cocaine has been found in shipments of lumber, chocolate, coffee, tropical fruit extract and lye.

FEES FROM OTHER SUPPLIERS

The leaders of the Cali group, with an organizational structure looser than Medellín's, take a percentage on shipments by smaller organizations in the area. In return, they provide such services as transportation, distribution in consumer nations and firepower in the war with the Medellín cartel.

The business rivalry flared into open warfare in the late 1980's, taking the lives of at least 200 people. Last September, Medellín gunmen shot to death 19 low-level Cali cartel employees on a ranch near here. Late in April, the Cali cartel struck back, exploding a grenade in a jail cell here, killing four Medellín men suspected of participating in the massacre.

But such high-profile incidents are more the exception for Cali. In general, its leaders have shunned headlines.

With Cali's aggressive surge into world markets, the Rodriguez brothers and their Cali colleague, Jose Santacruz Londono, are believed to be billionaires.

In contrast to Mr. Escobar, a high school graduate turned car thief, Gilberto Rodriguez Orejuela, 52 years old, is a former pharmacy manager who rose to preside over bank boards.

Known as "the chess player" for his astute moves, he favors business suits for his occasional forays into the local social scene. To help the next generation ease the family's fortune into legitimacy, his seven children attended college overseas, in the United States or Europe.

His brother, Miguel, is a 47-year-old lawyer who runs the family's legitimate businesses. These include real estate and Cali's champion club-soccer team, America.

The third member of the Cali triumverate, Mr. Santacruz, trained as an engineer. When he was denied admission at a local club, he built a replica in a rich suburban neighborhood.

MANY OPENINGS FOR ENTREPRENEURS

A lawyer explained how the traffickers have won friends and influence here. "They bought complicity," he said of the group's experiment with rogue capitalism.

"You gave a man $10,000. Two weeks later, he came back with $18,000. What part do you want to buy into? Flying paste from Bolivia? Flying the refined product to Mexico? Eight times in a row, you make money. The ninth time the plane goes down, and you take a loss."

Tuning his car radio to the local classical-music station, the lawyer set out for a late-night "narco-tour" through this city of 1.5 million.

"This house used to be the residence of the American consul," he said, pointing to a hillside estate with lush tropical vegetation spilling over a wall. "Now, it's a meeting place for Miguel Rodriguez. Isn't that ironic?"

U.S. OFFICIAL ISN'T AMUSED

In Washington, the paradox was lost on Mr. Bonner of the Drug Enforcement Administration. "Now that Escobar has surrendered," he said, "we would very much like to see a second front against the key players of the Cali cartel."

On the consumer end, New York authorities last month announced a defeat for Cali with the arrest of 20 trafficking suspects. "This was a heavy blow for the drug-trafficking cartel that operates from Cali, Colombia," Gov. Mario M. Cuomo said.

But so far, the drug war here has been mainly one of words.

Gilberto Rodriguez has indignantly protested Mr. Bonner's charges that he helped run "the most powerful criminal organization in the world today."

In a letter to Mr. Bonner in June, he wrote that "it is unfair to point to the Cauca Valley as the epicenter of drug trafficking in Colombia, and it is even more unfair when you pick out, without proof, Gilbert and Miguel Rodriguez as heads of the Cali cartel."

VELVET INTIMIDATION

Indeed, although there are trafficking charges against the Rodriguez brothers in the United States, Gilberto Rodriguez was cleared in a Cali court in 1986 of all charges against him. And under the country's new Constitution, the extradition of Colombians for trial overseas is banned. Without fear of extradition, Mr. Rodriguez says he remains in hiding only because the Medellín cartel wants to kill him.

On a recent afternoon, the Rodriguez public relations effort could be seen at a television station here. Two hours earlier, the station had broadcast charges from an American magazine that the Rodriguez brothers deal in cocaine. The telephone rang and, on recognizing the voice at the other end, the station's news editor visibly straightened in his chair.

"Yes sir, yes sir," he said, soothingly. "That tape was prepared in Bogotá and aired before we could see it here."

After the conversation ended, the editor, still visibly tense, said: "That was Gilberto Rodriguez. He said, 'I don't threaten. I only register complaints.' "

Colombia Marvels at Drug Kingpin: A Chain-Saw Killer, Too?

BY JAMES BROOKE | JUNE 21, 1995

BOGOTÁ, COLOMBIA, JUNE 20 — With his blazer, blue jeans, designer tie and engaging smile, Henry Loaiza Ceballos appeared on television today as if he were on his way to a summer cocktail party. Only one accessory — silver handcuffs — hinted at his underworld nickname, the Scorpion.

His new chaperones, Colombia's police, said today that behind the tortoise-shell eyeglasses was a ruthless cocaine trafficker who once directed his men to cut up 107 of his enemies with chain saws.

"The Cali cartel's minister of war" is how newspapers described the man who surrendered here on Monday night, one step ahead of a combined military and police force that last weekend raided his far-flung properties, including 30 luxurious ranches, Cali apartments and two Caribbean beach houses.

The surrender followed the capture 10 days earlier of Gilberto Rodriguez Orejuela, often seen as the chairman of the Cali cartel, a multibillion-dollar business that controls most of the world's cocaine trade.

Lawyers for another top leader of the Cali cartel, Helmer Herrera, are negotiating his surrender, according to Colombia's public prosecutor's office. Under Colombia's plea bargain system, traffickers who surrender can win sentence reductions.

"Of all the ones we are searching for, he is the most violent," Brig. Gen. Rosso Jose Serrano, the director of Colombia's national police, said of Mr. Loaiza in an interview this evening. He predicted that with Mr. Loaiza's surrender the Cali cartel would not wage a terror campaign against the Government.

With the Scorpion apparently losing his sting, Colombians today focused on the dapper 46-year-old prisoner. Once a rural bus driver,

Mr. Loaiza grew to become a living caricature of the rural Latin American oligarch.

For loyal peasants, Mr. Loaiza bestowed bottles of rum, sponsored beauty pageants and gave candy to their children at Halloween. For peasants who tried to form unions or for Indians who challenged his land claims, he gave them bullets and the chain saw.

"This is a man with a reputation not only for drug trafficking, but also for hideous murders, chain-saw murders," Robert Gelbard, the highest State Department official for international drug affairs, said today in a telephone interview from Washington. "It would really be a tragedy if he could get out of jail in a few years to enjoy all his wealth."

As a bus driver in the Cauca River area, 100 miles north of Cali, Mr. Loaiza got to know the pioneer cocaine traffickers who were setting up business in the 1970's. Entering a gang as a bodyguard, he quickly rose through the ranks, in part because of his business acumen, in part because of his ruthlessness.

In 1986, the police first seized packets of cocaine stamped with a curious new logo, a scorpion painted with a black body and red feet.

In the last decade, his jungle laboratories and cocaine plantations multiplied, along with his personal wealth. Today, Mr. Loaiza's scorpion brand can be found on his 5,000 head of cattle, on his Colombian walking horses, and on the bottom of his swimming pool at one of his 30 ranches.

As Mr. Loaiza became one of the biggest property owners in the region, the upstart trafficker took on the rights and duties of Latin America's landed aristocracy. In Venadillo, his base of operations, he paid for repairs to the local Roman Catholic church. To win the loyalty of the local peasantry, he bought a fleet of 30 buses and gave free rides to those who could not pay the fare. On Halloween, his employees would drive a ranch truck through the village, handing out candy to children.

For Venadillo's annual patron saint festival, he sponsored folk music shows and beauty contests. Holding court in front of the stage, he distributed free bottles of rum to warm up the audience. Judges soon learned to crown his favorites as queens. At one pageant, he gave new motorcycles to all contestants. When one woman said she did not want a motorcycle, he gave her a car.

One year, a contestant became pregnant with Mr. Loaiza's child. To smooth over any misunderstandings, he gave her parents a ranch.

Such largesse was not dispensed to his enemies.

In April of 1990, peasants in Trujillo, where he owned a ranch, talked of forming a rural union. Mr. Loaiza joined forces with corrupt local army officers. In a yearlong reign of terror, 107 suspected unionists and guerrilla sympathizers were rounded up, tortured and killed, according to court documents. As a warning to others, their bodies were cut up with chain saws and dumped in the Cauca River.

A local priest, Tiberio Jesús Hernández, complained of the tortures and disappearances. A few days later his decapitated and dismembered body was recovered from the river. A few weeks after the murders started, a local fruit picker, Daniel Arcila, traveled to Cali to report that local peasants were being tortured and murdered with water hoses, blow torches and chain saws. A judicial psychiatrist declared him "paranoid." A few weeks later he was arrested. He has never been seen again.

The murders so shocked Colombia that a multi-party Truth Commission ordered the Government to pay damages to the victims' families and to build a memorial to the dead. None of those tied to the murders have so far been sentenced.

Today, Colombians studying the photographs of the mild-mannered, congenial prisoner had a hard time reconciling his appearance with his notoriety as the cartel's Scorpion.

"He doesn't look like a hired killer or a paramilitary," marveled one newspaper here, La Prensa. "Anyone would say that he is a math teacher."

A Web of Drugs and Strife in Colombia

BY LARRY ROHTER | APRIL 21, 2000

NEARLY HALF THE world's supply of cocaine originates within 150 miles of this isolated Colombian military outpost on the Putumayo River. So when Lt. German Arenas and his anti-drug troops recently set out by boat, they knew that finding a target would be the easy part.

Four hours later, his squadron of young marines stopped and marched into the equatorial wilderness, guns at the ready. By nightfall, they had found three crude cocaine-processing laboratories in the jungle, more than 6,000 seedlings of a new, more potent variety of coca plant, a half-dozen large fields brimming with ripening coca bushes and four hapless peasants.

But after they destroyed as much as they could, arrested the peasants and headed back downriver, the soldiers left behind at least 200 more labs hidden in the dense, trackless jungle and thousands more acres of coca plants, visible from the air everywhere across southern Colombia.

Over all, to the growing alarm of the Clinton administration, which has been bankrolling much of the anti-drug fight here, coca production in Colombia has more than doubled in the past five years. Using recent satellite images, American officials estimate that the country now grows or processes more than 500 tons of cocaine a year, or some 90 percent of the world's supply, and that Putumayo and Caqueta provinces are responsible for two-thirds of that.

But here as in many parts of southern Colombia, the army and the police dare not send spray planes and helicopters to eradicate the fields because the instant they appear, the aircraft invariably draw ground fire from the Marxist guerrilla forces that thrive on the drug trade.

The principal rebel group, the 15,000-strong Revolutionary Armed Forces of Colombia, or F.A.R.C., has been fighting the government since the mid-1960's, financing their war for most of that time with kidnappings and extortions.

But that has changed sharply in recent years. With the smashing of the notorious Medellín and Cali cartels, the guerrillas gained greater access to a far more lucrative source of income: coca and heroin. Now the rebels provide protection and support to the dozens of smaller trafficking groups that have sprung up to replace the cartels, and they are earning, by the Colombian government's estimate, more than $1 million a day.

That, in turn, has blurred the lines of what was once painted in relatively simple terms as an ideological battle between a pair of left-wing insurgencies that enjoy almost no popular support and a flawed but functioning democracy. Along the way, the focus of the conflict has shifted so that while the government still controls most of the country's territory, the war itself is increasingly being fought over cocaine and heroin.

On one side is the popularly elected government of President Andres Pastrana and its thin and poorly trained security forces. On the other are the increasingly well armed and richly financed leftist guerrillas. Equally menacing are the right-wing death squads, which have a long history of collusion with elements of the Colombian military and are also dealing in drugs.

"It is the only self-sustaining insurgency I have ever seen," said Gen. Charles E. Wilhelm, who is responsible for Latin America as commander in chief of the United States Southern Command. "There is no Cuba in back of it; there is no Soviet Union in back of it. It is this delicate merger of criminals, narco-traffickers with insurgents."

After nearly a decade of trying with little success to give government forces the edge in this confrontation, the White House and Congress are on the verge of the biggest gamble yet: a $1.6 billion package over two years that would beef up anti-drug training for the Colombian police and military and provide them with better equipment, including more than five dozen helicopters.

Critics in the United States and in the region worry that Washington is embracing an unrealistic plan. They say that Colombia lacks a concrete strategy for quickly getting the job done, that attacking cocaine at the source will be more difficult in Colombia than it was in neighboring countries, and that ultimately American military advisers will be drawn into the broader war between the guerrillas and the government.

THE COMBATANTS
Coca Brings Shooting From Many Directions

In the jungle and the farming villages, the distinction that the Pentagon and the State Department try to draw between arming an anti-drug war and avoiding Colombia's long-running civil conflict is blurred. The drug trade finances both the leftist insurgents and their rivals, the paramilitary death squads, who often operate with the tacit support of Colombian Army units.

"When people are shooting at you, it is hard to determine their immediate affiliation," said William Ledwith, director of international operations for the United States Drug Enforcement Administration. "Does it really make a difference if you are attacked by the F.A.R.C., the E.L.N., by paramilitaries or by a gang of narcotics traffickers wanting to defend their laboratories?" he asked, using the acronyms for the guerrilla groups. "To me, all the bullets are the same."

The rapid expansion of coca production in Colombia is in large part a consequence of two developments. One is what is known as the "balloon effect" — the reappearance of a problem in a new place after it has been squeezed in another — which followed successful American-led campaigns against coca growers in Peru and Bolivia.

The other, more recent development was a crucial miscalculation by President Pastrana. Elected on the promise of ending the debilitating war against the guerrillas, he tried to lure them to the negotiating table in 1998 by granting the leading guerrilla group control over a chunk of territory larger than Massachusetts, Connecticut and Rhode

Island combined. The guerrillas quickly turned it into an armed protectorate and a coca-growing factory, and the peace talks have floundered.

The breakup of the powerful Medellín and Cali cartels — the D.E.A. once called the latter "the most dangerous criminal group in history" — was originally expected to cripple the Colombian drug business. But their demise actually served to spur coca cultivation in more remote regions of the country and to foster unholy alliances between new drug gangs on one side and the leftist guerrillas and paramilitary forces on the other.

Just five years ago, Putumayo and neighboring Caqueta province were perhaps the poorest and most neglected areas of the country. Today, they have become a paradise for coca growers, with more than 100,000 acres cultivated under the protection of the largest rebel group, F.A.R.C.

Colombian trafficking groups have not only pushed aside Peru and Bolivia, the traditional sources of raw coca leaf, but also have moved aggressively into the heroin business, replacing Southeast Asia and Afghanistan as the source of most of the heroin seized in the United States.

For the Colombian military, that is a formidable challenge.

Though the national armed forces look strong on paper, with more than 100,000 soldiers, barely a third of them are ready for fighting. Under a widely criticized law that reflects the class prejudice and favoritism that run through Colombian society, high school graduates are forbidden to participate in combat.

The Colombian 90th Marine Battalion, to which Lieutenant Arenas, 28, and his teenage soldiers belong, patrols more than 1,500 miles of waterways in a network of four major rivers with barely 1,000 men and a handful of boats.

"For an area like this, a thousand men is nothing," Lieutenant Arenas said as his gunboat, the A.R.C. Leticia, equipped with two cannons, two machine guns and a pair of grenade launchers, chugged up the Putumayo River, with only the sound of its motors breaking the quiet. "Even though my guys are motivated, skilled and happy to be here, they face a lot of limitations."

The situation on the ground in Colombia had been eroding throughout the 1990's. But in 1994, just as the F.A.R.C. was beginning its big advance, the Clinton administration's relations with the Colombian government went into a deep freeze after Washington received information that President-elect Ernesto Samper had accepted $6 million in campaign contributions from drug cartels.

Normal ties resumed with the election of Mr. Pastrana in 1998. But it was not until the F.A.R.C. launched a nationwide offensive that brought it within striking distance of Bogotá last July that the real dimensions of the crisis began registering in Washington.

Gen. Barry R. McCaffrey, the director of the White House's Office of National Drug Control Policy and before that the commander of American military forces in Latin America, was the first to visit, and immediately began pushing President Clinton for emergency aid. That pressure, along with the major rebel action in July, convinced the White House of the seriousness of the situation in Colombia.

"It is essential the Colombian government restore state authority in this crucial region," General McCaffrey said during a more recent visit to a military base where three new anti-narcotics battalions, trained and financed with American assistance, are being formed. "The rapid expansion of drug production in Colombia, almost entirely in zones dominated by armed illegal groups, constitutes a drug emergency."

The biggest single item in the administration's proposed assistance package, which has been approved by the House and is pending in the Senate, is 63 helicopters, divided between 33 Bell UH-1N models and 30 more modern Sikorsky UH-60L Blackhawks, which are equipped with night-vision equipment and special armor. As the guerrillas and traffickers are aware, once training programs for crews and the construction of hangars are taken into account, the earliest date for complete delivery of the American-supplied equipment would be late next year.

Nevertheless, the prospect that American aid may soon begin flowing clearly excites the weary soldiers here. "Tell them we need air support, like the police get for their operations," said Lt. Gustavo Lievano, the marine unit's second in command.

A sergeant wanted to know, "How much more money are they going to give us to buy intelligence from informants?"

Illustrating the shoestring nature of operations here, on this mission Lieutenant Arenas was relying on walkie-talkies he paid for out of his own pocket while in the United States last year. Sometimes, even having enough gasoline for boats can be a problem.

But to some in Washington, the prospect of increased American involvement in Colombia is viewed much more warily.

"Before we quadruple our military aid and embark on an open-ended, costly commitment, the Colombian government needs to come up with a workable strategy," said Senator Patrick J. Leahy, Democrat of Vermont. "And our own administration needs to explain in detail what its goals are, what it expects to achieve at what cost over what period of time, and what the risks are, both to the thousands of Colombian civilians who will be caught in the middle when the war intensifies and to our own military advisers there.

"The Colombian government wants a blank check. That is not going to happen."

On the Colombian side, a recent poll shows that a majority of Colombians favor American intervention.

"Pastrana has shown that he doesn't know how to deal with this situation," said Diego Bedoya Hurtado, a Bogotá accountant. "Only the Americans are going to be able to get us out this mess."

From the perspective of the Pastrana administration, however, the American aid package is only part of a broader effort. It hopes to combine American military aid with nearly $1 billion from European nations for social and economic programs, and loans from international organizations, making for a whopping $7.5 billion effort that mixes carrot and stick.

One additional concern, both in Andean capitals and in Washington, is that any success against coca cultivation in Colombia will inevitably lead to a resurgence of coca growing in Peru or Bolivia.

"The balloon effect in drugs is something that we are always looking at," said Mr. Ledwith, director of international operations for the D.E.A.

Coca growing in Peru and Bolivia has been cut by more than half following increased cooperation between their governments and the United States. Successful crop substitution programs are one reason, but Peruvian President Alberto Fujimori's policy of shooting down any drug plane flying over Peru has been a huge deterrent, as have stepped-up eradication efforts.

Thus the bulk of coca production has shifted to Colombia, where most of the processing and marketing operations were already located. Feeling relatively safe on their native soil, the coca-growing syndicates have invested heavily in developing more potent strains, some of which can be harvested in as little as 60 days.

Smaller, more vulnerable trafficking groups have gravitated toward insurgent-dominated areas like this one, paying a tax on their drug income to the guerrillas in return for protection from the Colombian government's anti-drug campaign.

In 1996, a United States intelligence summary concluded that while guerrilla units were selling protection "in virtually all departments where traffickers operate," only a few "probably are involved more directly in localized, small-scale drug cultivation and processing."

But that has changed dramatically over the past 18 months, since the Colombian government gave a chunk of territory to the F.A.R.C. That step in late 1998 was intended as a gesture of good faith to lure the rebels into peace negotiations.

Hopes that the long war with the leftist guerrillas could end were raised almost two years ago when Mr. Pastrana was elected as a peace candidate implicitly endorsed by the F.A.R.C.'s main leader, Manuel Marulanda.

Informal peace talks with the group began last year. But after Mr. Pastrana flew to San Vicente del Caguan, the largest town in the rebel-held zone, for the opening ceremonies, Mr. Marulanda delivered a calculated snub by failing to appear, sending subalterns instead and leaving Mr. Pastrana looking at an empty chair in front of television cameras and photographers.

Since then, the negotiations have repeatedly stalled, with the F.A.R.C. breaking off discussions every time the government refuses to bend to one of its demands, and the government eventually giving in. Though the agreement called only for military forces to withdraw, the F.A.R.C. has also driven mayors, judges and Roman Catholic priests from its zone.

THE PEOPLE
Ever-Present Violence Creates Nation of Fear

To the average Colombian, it appears that while the government and rebel negotiating teams quibble over procedural issues, the F.A.R.C. is building up its military might and its drug-trafficking capabilities.

As a result, cartoonists now routinely portray Mr. Pastrana as a shrunken figure too small for the presidential sash and his shirt and pants.

F.A.R.C. leaders quickly converted their area, bitterly referred to by locals as "Farc landia," into a major cocaine production center complete with airstrips for exporting the product. Now, the second largest left-wing guerrilla group, the Army of National Liberation, known by the Spanish acronym E.L.N., wants its own demilitarized zone.

In recent interviews in Caqueta, the province adjoining the F.A.R.C. haven, peasants — none of whom were willing to be identified — also complained of being ordered by local F.A.R.C. commanders to grow coca. Other peasant farmers in the region who were already cultivating coca say they are now forced to sell to a guerrilla-controlled monopoly at a price that is about half what their crop would have fetched on the open market a year ago.

The paramilitary death squads controlled by Carlos Castano and closely allied with elements of the Colombian Armed Forces have acted no differently. These paramilitary troops were originally protected by law, defending businesses and landholders from leftists guerrillas, and aiming their assaults at civilians they suspected of aiding the rebels.

The paramilitary units lost their legal status more than a decade ago, and moved heavily into the drug trade. Three years ago, the D.E.A. described Mr. Castano "as a major narcotics trafficker in his own right," and in a startling interview on Colombian television on March 1, the paramilitary chieftain acknowledged that the bulk of his group's money now comes from drugs.

As the conflict deepens, the situation for ordinary Colombians has grown worse. At least 35,000 people have been killed over the past decade, and more than 1.5 million people, most of them peasants, have been forced to leave their homes.

"First the paramilitaries came and told us to leave or they would kill us, and then when we were resettled, the guerrillas came and at gunpoint forced two of my sons to join them," said Javier Gonzalez, a refugee from Cordoba province in the northwest. "For the past three years, we have been sent from one place to the next, but everywhere we go, we are mistreated and abused."

In addition, at least 2 percent of Colombia's 40 million people — some 800,000 mostly middle-class people — have left the country since 1996, most of them for the United States. Investors are also fleeing in the face of extortion demands by guerrilla and paramilitary groups, and unemployment is at a record rate of one worker in five after a recession that shrank the economy by more than 5 percent last year.

A recent poll shows Colombians worry most about the pervasive violence that accompanies the drug crisis.

Colombia's murder rate is 10 times that of the United States, and its kidnapping rate is the highest in the world, thanks in large part to spectacular mass abductions like the E.L.N.'s raid on a Roman Catholic church service in Cali last year that resulted in more than 150 hostages.

"It feels like we are besieged, with an enemy just outside the castle walls waiting to pluck anyone who comes into their grasp," a doctor who lives in Cali said recently. "There is no longer anywhere you can go where you are safe."

More than five million people marched last fall in support of the "No Mas" civic foundation, which is demanding an immediate cessation of hostilities. But the leader of that movement, Francisco Santos, was forced to leave the country in mid-March after the F.A.R.C. threatened to kill him.

"There is a tendency to see the Colombian conflict as a table with two legs, the government versus the guerrillas," thereby ignoring the aspirations of civil society, Mr. Santos said recently in Miami.

THE HARD QUESTIONS
A Brief Intervention or a Prolonged Effort?

For the Clinton administration, the unraveling of the situation in Colombia has created an uncomfortable dilemma. While the United States is determined to diminish the flow of cocaine and heroin into American cities, especially with an election looming, it does not want to be pulled into what can only be a long, bloody and expensive campaign in Latin America's longest running guerrilla war.

"The situation on the ground in Colombia is increasingly complicated, but our policy is very straightforward," Brian E. Sheridan, the Defense Department coordinator for drug enforcement policy and support, said recently in testimony to a Congressional panel. "We are working with the Colombian government on counternarcotics programs. We are not in the counterinsurgency business."

But to Colombian military officers in the field, there is no such distinction. "To me, they are one and the same thing," Lieutenant Arenas said, clearly puzzled that anyone would suggest there is any difference between drug traffickers and guerrillas.

And while the Clinton administration is talking only of a two-year program, focused on the delivery of the helicopters and a training program for pilots, top Colombian military officials lay out a six-year campaign. They envision being able to break the F.A.R.C.'s control of coca-growing areas in the south in two years, after which the Colombian Armed Forces would focus on the Guaviare region in the country's heartland for two years and then northern areas dominated by paramilitary groups.

American officials contend that the only way the government can regain control of Putumayo and Caqueta provinces is through a coordinated effort in which the Armed Forces clean out guerrilla concentrations and are followed by police units that fumigate coca fields by air.

But very little in the battlefield record of the Colombian Army and Air Force inspires confidence in that kind of plan. Throughout the 1990's, the United States funneled most of its aid and training to the Colombian National Police because American officials regarded the Armed Forces as a bloated, corrupt and largely defensive force.

The American approach is also likely to exacerbate a longstanding debate about the most effective way to reduce drug cultivation. While aerial spraying is traditionally favored by the United States, many in Colombia argue that crop substitution programs similar to those that proved successful in Bolivia and Peru are more effective ways to wean peasant farmers from drug crops.

The aid package now before the United States Congress includes a hefty increase in financing for such "alternative development" programs, to $127 million over the next two years from $5 million in the last budget. But the experience of the National Plan for Alternative Development, the Colombian government's crop substitution agency, makes clear that coordinating aerial spraying and crop substitution programs requires a precision that has eluded American and Colombian experts.

Human rights groups see another, equally troubling problem in the White House aid package. They point to a long history of cooperation between some Colombian military units and Mr. Castano's right-wing death squads, or paramilitaries.

According to the Colombian prosecutor's office, the death squads killed nearly 1,000 people in more than 125 massacres in 1999. Recent reports by Human Rights Watch and the United Nations and investigations by Colombian prosecutors have singled out specific Colombian military units and commanders as having provided support to the death squads or having failed to heed calls for help from villages under attack.

To curb such abuses, Congress passed the Leahy Amendment in 1997, prohibiting the United States from providing assistance to any Colombian military unit that violates human rights. As a result, some Colombian battalions have been disqualified from receiving American aid, new units have been formed, and instruction in human rights has become a required part of Colombian military training. But critics of the Clinton administration's aid package insist not only that those restrictions be strengthened, but that new oversight mechanisms be included.

"The government paints a rosy picture, but the reality is that army officers who commit atrocities are almost never prosecuted," Senator Leahy, the author of the amendment, said recently.

"Links between the army and paramilitaries are widespread, and human rights investigators have had to flee the country."

R. Rand Beers, assistant secretary of state for international narcotics and law enforcement affairs, denied that paramilitary groups would get better treatment than their enemies on the left. "We are pressing the Colombian government to live up to the promise that they will go after the paras, and we will continue to do that," he said, referring to the paramilitary troops.

American policy, however, is to "go after the drugs wherever they are," Mr. Beers added. "We will start by going after the largest concentrations of those drugs, and right now that is in the south. So it's not that they are getting a free ride because they are paras. It's because the paras have fewer forces in the south than the F.A.R.C. at this time. That said, the paras are increasing their presence in the south, and are becoming a more significant problem there."

Even without the aid package, the United States' commitment in Colombia is already growing. The Colombian battalions patrol the rivers of southern Colombia in American-made Pirana vessels, and last year, a Riverine War School opened in Puerto Leguizamo with some classes by visiting American instructors.

"We've had your Coast Guard come in to show how to board vessels, your Army and Marines to teach combat on land and water, the Miami police to demonstrate detention methods," Lieutenant Arenas said enthusiastically. Many of the Americans leave equipment and supplies behind as gifts, a gesture that is deeply appreciated by troops who are short of everything from boots and maps to two-way radios.

At any given moment, 80 to 220 American military officials are working in Colombia, according to the United States Embassy in Bogotá. The largest concentrations are at Tolemaida in the center of the country, and Tres Esquinas in the southwest, where the first of three counternarcotics battalions was trained last year and two more battalions are scheduled to be formed this year.

All told, American aid to Colombia has grown by 3,500 percent since 1993, General McCaffrey said. That makes Colombia the largest recipient of American aid outside the Middle East even without the new flows of equipment and training under discussion.

Washington clearly hopes that this large one-time injection of new aid will prove sufficient for the Colombian government to regain the upper hand.

But Fernando Cepeda Ulloa, a former minister of the interior and ambassador to the United States, was speaking for many Colombians, and some Americans, when he recently suggested that a pair of fundamental questions remain.

"Is the elimination of narcotics trafficking the key to achieving peace, or is the achievement of peace necessary to the elimination of narcotics?" he asked. "That is a dilemma that has to be analyzed and contemplated."

Mexico's Drug Cartels Wage Fierce Battle for Their Turf

BY GINGER THOMPSON AND JAMES C. MCKINLEY JR. | JAN. 14, 2005

MEXICO CITY, JAN. 13 — Prisons have not contained the drug war.

In the last four years, Mexico has made unprecedented advances in its fight against drug cartels by capturing many of the country's most powerful kingpins. Now, however, a new wave of drug-related killings has made clear that cartel leaders have begun to regroup, and are waging deadly campaigns from Mexico's maximum security prison to keep control of their territories.

At least 34 people, including 3 federal agents and 2 journalists, have been assassinated since June in the struggle. The authorities are reporting alarming spikes in drug-related violence from Cancún in the south to cities along Mexico's northern border with the United States.

"The fact of having incarcerated them does not in any way guarantee that they will not commit acts of violence," said Mexico's assistant attorney general for organized crime, José Luis Santiago Vasconcelos. "They are always looking for ways to undermine and destroy legal systems, to destroy prison systems and surveillance systems to keep operating."

Law enforcement officials said that at the epicenter of the recent violence is a mercurial drug dealer named Joaquín (El Chapo) Guzmán Loera, who broke out of prison in January 2001 hidden inside a laundry truck, and now seems determined to seize this country's principal drug routes. While other cartels have been weakened by the arrests of their top leaders, Mr. Guzmán has rebuilt his organization, turned former foes into allies and moved to expand his territory.

The authorities said Mr. Guzmán had waged a war on two fronts, attacking the Gulf Cartel, which controls the eastern border crossings with Texas in the state of Tamaulipas, and the Arellano Félix organization, which controls the western border between Tijuana and El Paso.

Desperate to stop him, the leaders of those beleaguered cartels — once archenemies — have also formed an alliance, hired a team of former special forces officers as hit men and orchestrated vicious counterattacks from Mexico's principal maximum security prison, La Palma.

The authorities say Osiel Cárdenas Guillén, the leader of the Gulf Cartel who has been in prison since 2003, leads the fight against Mr. Guzmán. And they say he is joined by Benjamin Arellano Félix, the feared leader of the Tijuana cartel, who was arrested in 2002.

"What we have here is a merger, essentially," said John S. Fernandes, the special agent in charge of the Drug Enforcement Administration's San Diego office. "They are trying to solidify their forces."

The two imprisoned mob bosses are battling incursions from Mr. Guzmán and, to a lesser degree, from other leaders in the Ciudad Juárez cartel, among them Ismael (El Mayo) Zambada, Juan José (El Azul) Esparragoza and Vicente Carrillo Fuentes, law enforcement officials say. The realignment has produced a spate of revenge killings. In October, the authorities found five men believed to have been Mr. Guzmán's associates bound and shot execution-style in the border city of Nuevo Laredo. A note addressed to Mr. Guzmán was found with the bodies. It read, "Send more idiots like these."

A month later, nine bodies were found outside Cancún. Five of the bodies, including three federal agents, were found dumped in a field off the airport highway. The police reported that the victims had been bound, tortured and shot once in the head. Four other victims were found burned to death inside a car a few miles away. The murders stem from a struggle between Mr. Guzmán and Mr. Cárdenas over money-laundering operations in that tourist town, Mexican investigators said.

On New Year's Eve, Mr. Guzmán's brother, who was being held at La Palma, was shot several times at point-blank range in the prison visiting area. He was the second convicted drug dealer associated with Mr. Guzmán to be killed at La Palma within the last three months.

And just last weekend, four men were found murdered gangland-style in the southern town of Morelia while two others turned up dead in Tamaulipas state near the American border. Investigators say both incidents appeared to be drug-related shootings. In Tamaulipas, the killers left a note taunting "El Chapo" on the bullet-ridden bodies.

The authorities said at least two people had been killed each day so far this year in Mr. Guzmán's home state of Sinaloa, considered the Mexican capital of drug trafficking.

The violence has raised questions about President Vicente Fox's crackdown against drug traffickers, praised here and in the United States for capturing more than 100 drug traffickers, among them 15 most-wanted kingpins, and weakening the systems of protection that allowed them to operate with impunity.

Law enforcement officials here and in the United States say that the crackdown has so badly weakened the cartels that they have been forced into volatile alliances and rash attacks. They see the killings as the last spasm of organizations desperate to stay in business.

"They are breaking up," said Mr. Vasconcelos, the assistant attorney general. "They are trying to sustain their strength by whatever means. That is what we are seeing now."

Other experts on drug trafficking, however, say that the government's crackdown has done little to interrupt the flow of drugs through this country, nor to stem the corruption that allows drug traffickers to buy control of police and prisons.

In the wake of the increased law enforcement operations, these experts say, cartels have shifted alliances, and some have even begun operating in smaller units. But they have begun to bounce back, and so has the violence that comes with them.

"The good news is that the government of Mexico has arrested more kingpins and dismantled more cartels," said Jorge Chabat, an expert on organized crime at the Mexican research institute CIDE. "The bad news is that it means nothing. It hasn't stopped drugs from moving across the country. In fact, all it has done is created more violence."

Mr. Chabat added, "For many years, the United States complained that if Mexico did its job and put these kingpins in jail, then the drug war would end. But Mexico has done its job, and the war continues."

In a meeting with reporters on Thursday, Mr. Vasconcelos said the jailed drug bosses had used their lawyers to carry messages to operatives on the outside. He also said an untold number of guards had been bribed or threatened into cooperating.

At least five prison officials are being held in connection with the recent killings at the jail, including the director and two of his aides. And in the last week the government reinforced the security at La Palma, sending an additional 179 guards.

Jésus Blancornelas, a crusading Tijuana journalist who is one of the country's foremost experts on the drug trade, said adding officers to the prison would not change anything unless the rotten officers were removed.

"The problem in Mexico is that as long as you don't clean up the police, the drug trafficking system is going to continue working," Mr. Blancornelas said. "They say to me what do you have to do to capture the drug dealers, and I tell them, first, you have to capture the bad cops."

Mexico Sends 4 Kingpins to Face Trial in the U.S.

BY JAMES C. MCKINLEY JR. | JAN. 21, 2007

MEXICO CITY, JAN. 20 — Breaking with longstanding practice, Mexico extradited four major drug traffickers to the United States late Friday and sent a signal that the country's newly elected president, Felipe Calderón, is serious about cooperating with his northern neighbor to dismantle cartels.

United States law enforcement officials have long complained about Mexican reluctance to hand over drug traffickers indicted in crimes north of the Rio Grande, as many drug kingpins have continued to operate their deadly networks from inside Mexican prisons, where they have been able to corrupt officials.

Until now, however, the Mexican government has resisted the extraditions, arguing that the drug cartel leaders must face justice here first. Also, until a recent Supreme Court ruling, Mexican officials were unable to extradite criminals because they face the death penalty in the United States, which is banned in Mexico. The court overturned that rule.

"The actions overnight by the Mexican government are unprecedented in their scope and importance," the United States attorney general, Alberto R. Gonzales, said in a statement on Saturday.

Osiel Cárdenas Guillén, the leader of the Gulf Cartel in Tamaulipas State, was among the 21 people flown under heavy armed guard to the United States on Friday night and handed over to federal authorities. He is under indictment in Texas for trafficking in marijuana and threatening to kill three law enforcement agents.

The Mexican government also turned over Ismael and Gilberto Higuera Guerrero, brothers who were high-ranking members of the Arellano-Félix cartel in Tijuana, as well as Hector Palma Salazar, a former leader in the Sinaloa cartel. All face racketeering and drug trafficking charges in Southern California.

The Sinaloa cartel controls the border around El Paso. Joaquín Guzmán, known as El Chapo, escaped from prison in 2001 after bribing officials and still oversees the gang, along with several other important traffickers who have somehow eluded the Mexican police.

Former President Vicente Fox, who left office in December, created a special force to combat organized crime and arrested scores of high-ranking mobsters, weakening the three major cartels in Tijuana and Sinaloa State in the west and Tamaulipas State, along the eastern Texas border.

But his administration failed to break up the Sinaloa mob, and the arrests of people like Mr. Cárdenas and his counterpart in Tijuana, Benjamin Arellano-Félix, set off an underworld turf war that has increased in brutality and claimed thousands of lives in recent years.

Officials at the Drug Enforcement Agency privately voiced frustration with the Fox administration for not extraditing the drug kingpins to the United States, where they would be unable to run their networks from prison. A similar tactic proved effective in Colombia, Panama and other countries where drugs are produced and shipped.

Mr. Calderón and his attorney general, Eduardo Medina Mora, did not immediately say why they had switched course. The attorney general's office put out a statement saying simply that the people extradited had run out of appeals against extradition and that Mexico wanted them to face trial in the United States before the time limit ran out on the charges there.

But all are serving sentences or facing trials in Mexico. In the past, the Mexican authorities have said those were barriers to extradition.

A high-ranking federal prosecutor, speaking on the condition of anonymity, said President Calderón had decided to extradite the drug traffickers despite their pending legal proceedings. The aim is to make it difficult for them to communicate with their lieutenants in Mexico. "It breaks up the entire logistical structure of these organizations here," the prosecutor said.

Besides the four top drug traffickers, the Mexicans extradited seven other lower-level drug dealers, among them Gilberto Salinas Doria, who is wanted in the Southern District of New York on charges of helping to import 200 tons of cocaine.

They delivered four other prisoners wanted on charges of murder, drug trafficking and trafficking in prostitutes, officials said. One of these, Consuelo Carreto Valencia, is under indictment in New York City on charges of smuggling women and forcing them to become prostitutes.

In Mexico, a Fugitive's Arrest Captivates the Cameras

BY JAMES C. MCKINLEY JR. | OCT. 12, 2007

MEXICO CITY, OCT. 11 — A woman who succeeds in a field dominated by men is always intriguing to the public, but when that field happens to be big-time cocaine trafficking, and the woman is graced with both charm and beauty, a criminal celebrity is born.

Ever since her arrest last month, Sandra Ávila Beltrán, better known as the Queen of the Pacific, has been getting the kind of press here that would have made Jesse James envious. Mexicans are closely following the case against her and the efforts to extradite her to United States, where she is wanted in Florida.

Prosecutors here say Ms. Ávila Beltrán, a shapely, raven-haired, 46-year-old with a taste for high fashion, has played an important role in forging a federation of drug traffickers in western Sinaloa State as well as creating an alliance between them and Colombian suppliers.

Along the way, she seduced many drug kingpins and upper-echelon police officers, becoming a powerful force in the cocaine world through a combination of ruthless business sense, a mobster's wiles and her sex appeal, prosecutors say.

It is a measure of her importance in the Mexican underworld that some Tijuana musicians have written a song in her honor. This "narco-corrido" extols her virtues as "a top lady who is a key part of the business." It has been played over and over on radio stations since her arrest.

The police say Ms. Ávila Beltrán was born into the trade. She is the niece of Miguel Ángel Félix Gallardo, an important trafficker from Guadalajara serving a long sentence for smuggling and the murder of an American drug-enforcement agent, Enrique Camarena. Another uncle is Juan José Quintero Payán, who was extradited to the United States recently on drug smuggling charges. Her list of romantic conquests, the police say, include important members of the Sinaloa cartel like Ismael Zambada, known as El Mayo, and Ignacio Coronel, known as Nacho, investigators say. Both remain powerful leaders in the Sinaloa organization.

Her lovers have fared better than her legal husbands. She was at one time married to José Luis Fuentes, the commander of the federal police in Sinaloa, who was executed gangland style. Later she married Rodolfo López Amavizca, the commander of the National Institute for the Combat Against Drugs, which is now defunct. He was also murdered in 2000 by a gunman in a hotel in Hermosillo, the capital of northwestern Sonora State.

Of all her love affairs, however, it was her longtime union with a reputed Colombian trafficker, Juan Diego Espinosa, who calls himself the Tiger, that cemented her position in the upper echelons of the Mexican underworld.

Together, the two of them forged deals between Mexican and Colombian traffickers in the late 1990s and in 2000. She took control of shipping cocaine from the North Valley Cartel in Colombia to ports in western Mexico, thus earning her name the Queen of the Pacific.

At the same time, Ms. Ávila Beltrán established several legitimate businesses that investigators suspect were used to launder money — a string of tanning salons and a thriving real estate company with more than 200 properties in Sonora State.

But her luck began to run out in December 2001, when the authorities seized a tuna boat, the Macel, in the port of Manzanillo and found more than nine tons of cocaine aboard, worth $80 million.

Six months later, her teenage son was kidnapped in Guadalajara, and she slipped up. She contacted the authorities for help. She eventually asked the police to stay out of the way, handled the negotiations with the kidnappers herself and got her son back after 17 days.

But prosecutors say the $5 million ransom request raised their suspicions about her income. They started investigating her, and by July 2002 had found evidence linking her to the Macel shipment. They also linked her to other members of Mr. Espinosa's family, among them a woman who was arrested at the Mexico City airport carrying about $1.5 million, prosecutors say.

Ms. Ávila Beltrán eluded arrest and went underground. She lived quietly in Mexico City with Mr. Espinosa in a middle-class neighborhood and went by the name Daniela García Chavez.

She did not drop her taste for luxury. She was fond of dining at Chez Wok, an expensive Thai restaurant in the Polanco neighborhood. She drove a BMW and frequented hair salons favored by television celebrities.

In March 2004, she was indicted on separate drug smuggling charges in Miami along with several members of the Espinosa family, according to court documents. But United States agents made no headway toward her arrest, even though she was living a high-profile lifestyle in Mexico City, court documents said.

Eventually, last year, a United States judge ordered arrest warrants for two other defendants be quashed in an effort to get them to cooperate and help to locate Ms. Ávila Beltrán. The judge pointed out that she had been a fugitive in Mexico for years.

On Sept. 28, more than 30 Mexican federal agents swarmed into a diner where she was having coffee and arrested her. She coolly asked the agents to let her freshen her makeup before the police filmed her transfer to jail. On the videotape, she tosses her hair and smiles for the camera, strutting in tight jeans and spiked heels, on the arm of an agent.

In a later tape of her being questioned by the police, she describes herself as a housewife who earns a little money on the side "selling clothes, houses." Asked why she had been arrested, she responds with nonchalance: "Because of an extradition order to the United States."

Though some local press reports said the federal case against her was weak, a judge last week ordered her arrested. She responded with her trademark insouciance at a hearing where charges related to the Macel shipment were recited for the record. "I already know them by heart," she noted.

Sandra Ávila Beltrán, dubbed the Queen of the Pacific, after she was arrested by federal agents outside a restaurant in southern Mexico City.

Her life behind bars at the Santa Martha Acatitla women's prison in the capital has apparently not been to her liking. She filed a complaint with a Mexico City human rights commission, saying her cell had insects, which she referred to as "noxious fauna." She also said the ban on bringing in food from restaurants violated her rights.

The Long War of
Genaro García Luna

BY DANIEL KURTZ-PHELAN | JULY 13, 2008

WHEN GENARO GARCÍA LUNA, Mexico's top police official, arrived in Tijuana in January, the city was in the middle of a storm of violence that he found, as he put it to me with clipped understatement soon after his visit, "surprising." First, three local police officers were murdered in a single night, apparently in retaliation for a bust that a drug-cartel boss warned them not to carry out. A few days later, federal police officers tried to storm a trafficker safe house in a quiet Tijuana neighborhood and ended up in a shootout. Five gunmen held off dozens of police officers and soldiers for more than three hours. By the time the police made it inside the house, six kidnap victims from a rival cartel being held there had been executed. The traffickers had skinned off some of the victims' faces to conceal their identities.

The attacks on the police officers were particularly worrying for García Luna, who as secretary of public security is one of the officials in charge of implementing President Felipe Calderón's decision to aggressively wage war on drug trafficking. Just before García Luna's visit to Tijuana, a police officer's wife and 12-year-old daughter were murdered in their home there, in violation of a longstanding code of combat that is supposed to safeguard the families of cops and traffickers alike. In a further gesture of defiance, cartel assassins were issuing death threats over the police force's own radio frequency, and the cartel seemed to be getting inside information about police operations. The gunmen in the Tijuana shootout had a cache of automatic weapons, including AK-47's, the traditional weapon of choice for the cartels. During the shootout, the police, unsure of their ability to control the crossfire, evacuated hundreds of children from an adjacent preschool. "People are saying, 'There are children fleeing here, like it's Iraq,' " García Luna told me later.

Genaro García Luna, the general in the latest, possibly most-violent war on drugs.

What was "surprising" to him, however, was not the firepower or brutality of the traffickers; the surprising thing was that in Tijuana, the government was supposed to be *winning*. Over the previous few years, the city's dominant drug cartel, known as the Arellano Félix cartel, after the family that runs it, had been, as many of García Luna's top aides told me, practically dismantled. One of the Arellano Félix brothers was shot, another arrested by Mexican special forces and a third seized by American agents as he fished in the Pacific from a boat called the Dock Holiday. U.S. and Mexican authorities shut down several "narcotunnels," elaborately engineered smuggling passages that run as deep as 100 feet below the fence that separates Tijuana from the United States. Stash after stash of cocaine, heroin, methamphetamine and marijuana was seized in town or intercepted at the border.

But by the measure that matters most to the average citizen — security — the situation was as bad or worse than ever. Even as the Mexican government was sending fleets of security officers to Tijuana, there were at least 15 drug-related killings there the week of García Luna's visit.

This pattern has become common in Mexico. Since the end of 2006, the Calderón government has sent more than 25,000 soldiers and federal police on high-powered anti-drug "operations" to combat drug cartels. It has initiated sweeping plans for judicial and police reform. It has extradited several top cartel figures to the United States, earning praise and a package of anti-drug aid from the U.S. government. Yet this year is on pace to be the bloodiest on record for Mexico's drug war, surpassing by almost 50 percent last year's toll of more than 2,500 deaths.

Soon after the Tijuana shootout, the police got a tip about another building nearby — a plain-looking house with pale yellow walls and a basketball hoop outside. They raided it and found an underground chamber that they called an "assassin training school." A policeman in a black ski mask gave me a tour, guiding me down a wooden ladder hidden beneath a fake bathroom sink. It went down into a long room with a low ceiling and lined with thick black insulation. There was heavy equipment for outfitting and repairing guns, and an estimated 30,000 rounds of ammunition were neatly organized by caliber on gray plastic shelves. Used shooting targets were pinned up to metal cans filled with scraps of tire, and hundreds of shells littered the floor. "It is incredible, facing these weapons," García Luna told me later, shaking his head. "It is truly astonishing, in terms of quantity, in terms of caliber. Before, the most powerful weapon we would find was the cuerno de chivo" — the goat's horn, Mexican slang for an AK-47. "Now we're finding grenades, rockets."

Since taking over as Mexico's top cop at the end of 2006, García Luna has repeatedly said the situation with the drug cartels would get worse before it got better. But when I spoke to him after his visit to Tijuana, even he seemed startled at just how bad the violence had become — especially since the narcos had started turning their weapons on the state instead of on one another. One of García's Luna's top lieutenants, the federal police chief Edgar Millán Gómez, told me in March, "We are seeing a response to our operations: more attacks on police." A month and a half later he, too, was dead.

A FEW WEEKS AFTER the Tijuana bust, I went with García Luna to a meeting of state commanders and some local police chiefs outside Acapulco. The city has suffered its own bouts of drug violence in recent years. It is a major entry and distribution point for Colombian cocaine, and for much of last year two rival cartels were fighting for the turf. Acapulco has become famous for beheadings. In one notorious case, the heads of two police officers were deposited in front of a government building, along with a hand-lettered sign that read, "So that you learn some respect." We traveled to the site of the meeting, an upscale beachfront hotel filled with American tourists, under the guard of gunmen in armored black S.U.V.'s.

Although he was just 38 when Calderón tapped him for his current job, García Luna had already spent almost 20 years in the security services, much of it monitoring organized crime and drug trafficking. By his late 20s, he was considered something of a wunderkind. Trained as an engineer, he was savvy about and comfortable with new technology at a time when those skills were becoming valued in security circles, and he rose quickly through the ranks. In the late '90s, as Mexico began to emerge from 70 years of one-party rule, García Luna became a central player in efforts to reform the police. He helped found a new "preventive" police charged with keeping order throughout the country, then headed up the new Federal Investigation Agency, or AFI. Both these organizations are now functionally under his command, and if he has his way they will become an integrated federal police force in the coming years.

Raúl Benítez Manaut, a security analyst at the National Autonomous University of Mexico, calls García Luna's task "the hardest job in the country." For now, in carrying out many of the biggest operations against the cartels, the government has relied on the Mexican military. But militarization carries risks. The military worries about increasing corruption and a growing number of soldiers deserting their units to join the traffickers; others have warned that militarization will lead to major human rights violations. García Luna recently announced that the military should be heading back to the barracks, and a new and improved police — better-armed, better-trained, less corrupt — should begin fighting on its own by the end of this year. Before that can happen, though, he will have to build a kind of cohesive and effective federal police force that Mexico has never had.

At the meeting in Acapulco, the police chiefs, tough-looking men with mustaches and wearing guayabera shirts, were waiting for García Luna, their boss, in a conference room. With his square jaw, squat build and crew cut, García Luna cultivates the image of a cop in a world of politicians, a doer in a world of talkers, and after a cursory welcome he quickly moved to the matter at hand. He wanted to discuss, he said, "combating corruption through the systematic purging of the police corps." That would mean "cleaning up" the forces controlled by some of the men in the room — with their help if possible, "by force if necessary."

Local police forces — which make up the vast majority of police in Mexico — are the "Achilles' heel of Mexican security," as Jorge Chabat, a security expert close to the government, puts it. In much of the country the police are popularly viewed as abusive, incompetent and corrupt — a perception not helped by periodic scandals, like the recent appearance of videos showing Mexican police officers being trained in torture methods. In some of the main trafficker strongholds, the police are the protectors of the cartels; U.S. Drug Enforcement Administration officers on the ground refuse to even interact with local police departments for fear that doing so will put them at risk. David Zavala, a federal police commander running García Luna's operation in the border city of Juárez, told me: "When we arrived, we first had to get the municipal police out of the way. A lot of them are involved in trafficking. Sometimes they'll tell us, 'There's nothing over there.' That's the first place we look."

The system of local law enforcement in Mexico has been "abandoned," García Luna told me. "There is no strategy. Wages are very low. There is no trust." Corruption among police officers, he went on, "is part of their everyday life." García Luna has resorted to a variety of measures to bring the nation's police in line, and he was explaining them to the police chiefs in Acapulco. To get their share of the $300 million the government has for improving local law enforcement, he said, the local departments will have to start working with a new national crime and intelligence system and subject their officers to a regimen of "trust tests" — polygraph exams, financial audits, psychological evaluations. Until then, as many of the chiefs knew from experience, García Luna would not hesitate to use more extreme measures, including forcibly disarming suspect officers.

After the meeting, I joined García Luna as he went to the hotel bar to have a beer with a police commander. García Luna said he thought the meeting had gone well, but he seemed more interested in talking about bomb design. The week before, a homemade explosive device had gone off in the center of Mexico City, killing the man carrying it and wounding a woman who was with him. The word was that the bomb was intended for a police official's car as retribution for a series of strikes against the so-called Sinaloa cartel — signaling, many feared, a new phase in the drug war. Mexican security experts were talking about "Colombianization" or "the Pablo Escobar effect" — the idea being that, as with Escobar in Colombia in the late '80s and early '90s, the cartels were responding to the crackdown with a no-holds-barred assault on the state. "Now, in 2008, we are reaching terrorist violence," Samuel González Ruiz, a former head of the Mexican attorney general's organized-crime unit, told me the day after the explosion. "It is an escalation in their fight against the authorities."

But escalation was not the cartel's only tactic. Reports were filtering out of Tijuana that, in the wake of the shootout there, representatives of the Arellano Félix cartel had offered police and military officials a pact: the cartel would agree to control violence if the authorities would agree to let the cartels do business. The offer leaked to the press, prompting speculation about whether the government might negotiate.

The mere suggestion of a negotiation made García Luna angry. "Look, I'll tell you with all forcefulness, we are not going to make a pact with anyone," he said. "We are obligated to confront crime. That is our job, that is our duty, and we will not consider a pact." And with that, he changed the subject.

UNTIL QUITE RECENTLY, however, pacts between the government and the cartels, spoken or unspoken, were the norm. For most of the 20th century, Mexico was ruled by the Institutional Revolutionary Party. The P.R.I. was authoritarian and corrupt, but these traits offered certain advantages when dealing with the drug trade. Political power was centralized and tightly controlled. For a cartel, buying off a key figure in the P.R.I. was enough to guarantee dominance on a patch of territory. In exchange, the cartel had to keep the killing at a tolerable level and to stay off other cartels' turf. Having accepted the drug trade's existence, the government could act as an arbiter and as a check on violence. These arrangements were what García Luna refers to as "the historical laws of corruption" — and they are precisely what he sees as his task to break.

"In some cases," Jeffrey Davidow, the U.S. ambassador to Mexico in the final years of the P.R.I., told me, "there was absolute corruption, in the sense that the cartels would go to the governor or a mayor and say, 'Here's the money, don't bother us.' In other cases, and this might have been more common, the cartels would say, 'Look, we're going to do business here — don't bother us, and we won't bother you.' It was a matter of reaching accommodation. There were reports that if the cartel had to kill anyone, they would take that person across state lines and kill them in the neighboring state."

In the latter half of the '90s, Mexico's one-party political system started to open up, and in the 2000 presidential election, the P.R.I. lost power to Vicente Fox, a former Coca-Cola executive running under the banner of the National Action Party. The transition to democracy was a moment of great hope for Mexico. But it also undermined the system of de facto regulation of the drug trade. "What happened," explains Luis Astorga, a Mexican scholar who studies the history of drug trafficking, "is that the state ceased being the referee of disputes and an apparatus that had the capacity to control, contain and simultaneously protect these groups. If there is no referee, the cartels will have to resolve disputes themselves, and drug traffickers don't do this by having meetings."

García Luna became a key player in Mexico's antidrug efforts while this transition was taking place. "When we went in, we staked everything on taking on the heads of the criminal structure, going after the bosses," he told me. The government has captured or killed some of the top figures in the Mexican cartels — several of the Arellano Félix brothers of Tijuana, Alfredo Beltrán Leyva of Sinaloa and Osiel Cárdenas Guillén of the Gulf cartel, which dominates the border towns abutting southeastern Texas. "The idea," García Luna said, "was that by taking off the head, the body would stop functioning." Instead, he noted ruefully, "the assassins took control."

Rather than destroying the cartels, the government's high-level strikes transformed the cartels from hierarchical organizations with commanding figures at the top to unruly mobs of men vying for power. The cartel's hit men and hired muscle began shooting and slaughtering their way into the upper ranks of the organizations. "The government has gotten rid of some of the old bosses, but now we've got ourselves new leaders who are less sophisticated and more violent," a top Mexican intelligence official, who was not authorized to speak publicly, told me.

There have also been changes in the drug trade itself. As Mexico has grown more prosperous, domestic drug use — driven in part by cartel employees who are paid in product — has grown considerably. Trafficking patterns have shifted as well. As Colombian cartels were weakened by a U.S.-backed government crackdown starting in the 1990s, and Caribbean routes became riskier for traffickers, Mexicans started taking over — just as a Nafta-induced trade boom made it easier than ever to get drugs across the border. The Mexican cartels long ago replaced the Colombians as the dominant players in the global cocaine trade. Now, according to U.S. government figures, about 90 percent of the cocaine consumed in the United States enters by land from Mexico.

WHEN I MET GARCÍA LUNA in Washington in January, soon after the shootout in Tijuana made headlines in the United States, he was carrying with him a manila envelope full of color photographs. The photographs were grisly full-color shots of dead Mexican police and narco gun caches — a police officer bleeding on the ground; the aftermath of the shootout; the underground firing range. García Luna thought of them as a sort of secret weapon of his own.

García Luna was in Washington to make the rounds of U.S. government agencies and Congressional offices — visiting those who would have to approve and implement the Merida Initiative, a $1.4 billion package of counternarcotics aid that the Bush administration proposed. (Congress has since authorized $400 million worth of aid to Mexico for next year, including equipment and technical support for García Luna's police.) Seeming out of his element in the government buildings and think tanks — unlike many powerful Mexicans, he does not speak much English (all of my interviews with him were conducted in Spanish) — García Luna met with government officials and diplomats and gave a stilted power-point presentation to policy experts. He seemed more interested in the photographs he had brought, his way of making a blunt point about a touchy aspect of U.S.-Mexican relations: the vast majority of weapons in the cartel's arsenals (80 to 90 percent, according to the Mexican government's figures) are purchased in the United States, often at loosely regulated gun shows, and smuggled into Mexico by the same networks that smuggle drugs the opposite direction. García Luna has a hard time concealing his anger about the fact that U.S. laws make it difficult to do much about this "brutal flow" of firepower. "How is it possible," he asked me, "that a person is allowed to go buy a hundred *cuernos de chivo*" — AK-47's — "for himself?" In the United States, he said, "there was a lot of indifference."

In meetings with U.S. officials, García Luna passed around the photographs, with little fanfare or preface. Davy Aguilera, the Mexico attaché for the Bureau of Alcohol, Tobacco and Firearms, who was present for one of García Luna's presentations, said that the images of gun violence "made a real impression inside the Beltway." Many U.S. officials have come to share García Luna's frustration. "You take the guns away and you'll win," a senior Senate staff member who worked on the Merida Initiative (and who is not authorized to talk publicly about legislation that came out of his committee) said to me. "But if you can't deal with the issue of guns, you're not going to see much progress. They're finding unopened boxes of AK-47's."

García Luna told me that "the most important thing is co-responsibility" — an acknowledgment that the United States owes Mexico its support in a long and difficult war. The point of this acknowledgment is not just symbolism. The narcos, he explained, "terrorize the community to build their own social base through intimidation, through fear, so that they can carry out their criminal activities with impunity." U.S. support would help bolster the message that the good guys will not back down. Projecting toughness and resolve, as García Luna sees it, may be the most important weapon of all.

The cartels seem to understand this way of thinking, and they try to send the opposite message: the bad guys will never back down, either. In 2005, they started posting videos of gangland executions on YouTube. It was, García Luna and others have argued, a gimmick copied directly from insurgents in Iraq. "It was truly brutal. There was postproduction, editing, special effects," he pointed out. "These were not just videos meant to show what had happened." They were, rather, shots in the media war, meant to grab headlines and persuade the Mexican people that resistance is futile. It did not help the government's cause that some of the videos seemed to show the involvement of the police in cartel executions — including police officers operating under García Luna's command.

García Luna generally wins praise for acknowledging just how central police corruption is to the drug trade. He has ordered a substantive overhaul of the police, including new educational requirements and higher salaries for incoming officers. He has removed almost 300 federal police commanders, replacing them with trusted officers trained at a new police academy. U.S. counternarcotics officials tend to view the key people under García Luna's command as an honest core that can be trusted with U.S.-acquired intelligence. That improved intelligence-sharing has led to some high-profile successes in the past year: the seizure of more than 23 tons of cocaine, the biggest bust ever; the arrest of a legendary cartel figure known as the Queen of the Pacific; the discovery of $207 million in supposedly methamphetamine-related cash stashed in the walls of a Mexico City home. "The intel sharing has been key in all of those," Steve Robertson, a D.E.A. special agent who works on Mexico, told me.

Still, the sheer amount of money involved makes some police corruption as well as other high-level corruption almost inevitable. U.S. and Mexican observers alike are quick to hedge their praise of García Luna's efforts, often with a bit of history. In 1997, Mexico's newly appointed drug czar, an army general named Jesús Gutiérrez Rebollo, was arrested for working with the Juárez cartel. For months before that, he was celebrated as the tough, honest new face of Mexican counternarcotics.

"IN TAMAULIPAS, you never know who is with you and who is against you." Edgar Millán, the federal police chief, made this pronouncement as we drove through a scrubland of farms, factories, fast food and truck traffic in the state, which lies just across the border from South Texas. Conveniently for the cartels, Tamaulipas also has a major port on the

Gulf of Mexico. Cocaine comes to Mexico by sea, stashed in cargo from South or Central America, and then is smuggled into the United States in one of the millions of private vehicles or shipping containers that cross every year. In a single day, thousands of cars and trucks enter the United States from Tamaulipas alone. Enough cocaine to supply American demand for a year, a market worth some $35 billion, might fill a dozen or so tractor-trailers.

Tamaulipas has been one of the bloodiest fronts in Mexico's war on drugs for several years. And as in Tijuana, this year started out on a bad note. "We had to show the cartels that the Mexican state was not going to back off," Millán told me as we rode along the U.S. border in an armored pickup truck. We were in the middle of what is considered the stronghold of the Zetas, a group of former Mexican special-forces operatives who formed a paramilitary cell for the Tamaulipas-based Gulf cartel. The Zetas had become the most feared force in Mexico. "For them, this zone was untouchable," Millán said. "We practically couldn't come here." Several years ago, Mexico captured the Gulf cartel's boss, Osiel Cárdenas, and proclaimed a major victory. But that only left the Zetas to run the business on their own and made the rival Sinaloa cartel think it might have an opportunity to move into Tamaulipas. As a result, the Zetas were warring among themselves for control while also trying to fend off Sinaloa operatives.

When we got to the small border town of Río Bravo, Millán directed his driver to go to a former cartel safe house, near where the police engaged in a lengthy shootout with Zeta gunmen at the beginning of this year. Millán pointed out locations where bodies had fallen and grenades had landed. He hardly thought it worth noting that the safe house is directly across the street from the local police station. When I asked him about it, he shrugged. "The power and money of the cartels allows them to recruit police at every level," he said. "Local police forces have the most contact, the most presence in the streets, so they are the most infiltrated." Local taxi drivers also serve as a statewide surveillance network for the cartels, Millán explained.

Despite the poor start to the year, by spring García Luna was holding up Tamaulipas as evidence of what his strategy could achieve. Millán agreed that, after months of a heavy federal police and military presence — of checkpoints on the main highways, of targeted raids on suspected cartel houses, of "neutralizing" corrupt local police commanders — things had improved. "We have retaken the area," Millán told me. We stopped at a police checkpoint, where officers searched cars while half a dozen men with assault rifles looked on. "It continues to be dangerous, it continues to be difficult," he said. "But our commitment is clear. We are going to win this war." He summoned the commander overseeing the checkpoint, who explained how the police presence has affected the behavior of the cartels. "Now they are operating with a lower profile," he said. I asked him what that meant. "It doesn't mean they are stopping their business," he responded. "They are always looking for new strategies." The police have driven them off the main roads, so "they are using the dirt roads in the fields" to continue trafficking.

Later, I asked García Luna if this was an acceptable definition of success in the war on drugs: violence down, the police seemingly in charge, the cartels operating less conspicuously and less violently. He ducked the question but did not dispute the implication. "Given the temptation," he said, "there are people who are always going to play the game, whether by airplane or helicopter, by land, by sea, because there is a real market. … There is no product like it in the world." (When I asked David Johnson, the assistant secretary of state for International Narcotics and Law Enforcement, about the reason for mounting drug violence in Mexico, he said, without prompting, "In significant measure, it grows out of violent people taking advantage of the continuing strong demand in the United States.") García Luna mentioned Colombia, invoking an analogy that Mexican and U.S. officials generally resist. Colombia has received billions of dollars in U.S. anti-drug aid under Plan Colombia, and violence has fallen significantly in the past several years. "Do you know how much the amount of drugs leaving Colombia has gone down?" García Luna asked me. "Check," he said with a smile. And indeed, by all evidence, there has been no significant decrease in drug flows out of Colombia or in the availability of cocaine or heroin in the United States — and yet, Colombia is considered a success story.

In a recent interview with a member of the editorial board of The Wall Street Journal, Mexico's attorney general, Eduardo Medina Mora, acknowledged that the objective "cannot be destroying narcotrafficking or drug-related crime." "Trying to get rid of consumption and trafficking," he said, "is impossible." Jorge Chabat explained to me: "The strategy of the government is to turn the big cartels into lots of small cartels. If you have 50 small cartels instead of four big cartels, first you have less international pressure, and second, you will have violence in the short term, but in the long term you will have much less violence."

Achieving even that goal means changing the balance between the government and the cartels — and that may be a much bloodier task than García Luna and many Mexicans anticipate. The police have uncovered plots against top law-enforcement officials in Mexico City involving grenades and rocket launchers. The attorney general's office recently released statistics showing that under Calderón's government, almost 500 law-enforcement personnel — some of them clean, some of them surely corrupt — have been killed in drug violence. One border police chief even sought asylum in the United States. And in recent polls, Mexicans have expressed growing doubt that the authorities are up to the fight: 56 percent say they believe that the cartels are more powerful than the government, while just 23 percent say they believe the government is more powerful than the cartels. But García Luna and his men contend that they will not back down until the cartels have been broken. As Millán told me in Tamaulipas, "They think we will step back, but on the contrary, we will attack them harder."

A FEW WEEKS LATER, Millán was shot to death in an apartment in Mexico City. A disgruntled former federal cop had reportedly sold information about Millán's movements to the Sinaloa cartel. Two other federal police officials close to García Luna were also killed around the same time; another senior officer and his bodyguard were gunned down in June while eating lunch in Mexico City.

I asked García Luna recently whether the fight was worth it, for him personally and for Mexico. "This has been my life," he said, suggesting that such a calculation was not possible for him: he will fight because that is what he does. "I have been chosen to live this," he went on. "I have 20 years of it, and this position is the summit of my career. I feel a personal obligation." García Luna argues that Mexico is in a moment of violent transformation and that the only way through is to keep pushing forward. To Americans, he likes to bring up the example of the Mafia, to show that this has nothing to do with Mexican incompetence or corruption. "That is how it has been all over the world," he said. "Look at Chicago, New York, Italy."

García Luna had begun repeating the same phrase Millán used, which has turned into something of a mantra — *ni un paso atrás*, "not a step back." When I asked him about when violence would begin to decline, he became frustrated. "Is it costly?" he said. "Yes, it is costly. You have to face it." Over his shoulder was a small statue of Don Quixote, which he keeps on a shelf behind his desk.

DANIEL KURTZ-PHELAN is a senior editor at Foreign Affairs.

Drug Kingpin Is Captured in Mexico Near Border

BY RANDAL C. ARCHIBOLD | JULY 15, 2013

MEXICO CITY — The leader of one of Mexico's most violent and feared drug organizations, the Zetas, was captured Monday in a city near the Texas border, an emphatic retort from the new government to questions over whether it would go after top organized crime leaders.

The man, Miguel Ángel Treviño Morales, 40, who goes by the nickname Z-40 and is one of the most wanted people on both sides of the border, was detained by Mexican marines Monday morning, Mexican officials said at a news conference Monday night.

He was detained about 3:45 a.m., without a shot being fired, as he traveled in a pickup truck near Nuevo Laredo, opposite Laredo, Texas, with two other men who were also detained, the officials said, adding that the marines seized $2 million in cash and weapons.

Mr. Treviño was ranked among the most ruthless crime bosses, wanted for murder, organized crime, and torture; he has been linked to the killing and disappearance of 265 migrants in northeastern Mexico, including 72 found dead in August 2010.

He also faces drug and gun charges in the United States, which has offered a $5 million reward for information leading to his capture.

Eduardo Sánchez, the spokesman on security matters for the Mexican government, declined to say what role the United States played in the capture, though American law enforcement tips have often been behind high-profile arrests.

An American law enforcement official declined to provide details, deferring to the Mexican government announcement of the arrest, which was first reported by The Dallas Morning News on its Web site.

The Zetas operate primarily in Mexico, but their drug trafficking and organized crime violence have spread to other countries, and they have been known to recruit members in Texas and even to launder money through the quarter-horse industry in the United States.

Started by former soldiers and once the enforcement arm of another large cartel, the gang is known in Mexico for its brutality, and its members' calling card is often beheaded victims, body parts on highways and bodies hanged from bridges.

Mr. Treviño is the highest-ranking and most-sought-after drug capo arrested by the government of President Enrique Peña Nieto of Mexico, whose aides had questioned the so-called kingpin strategy of his predecessor, which had emphasized high-profile arrests. The leadership voids, battles for turf and confrontations with Mexican forces all sent violence soaring in the past several years, with tens of thousands dead or missing.

The new government had scoffed at the deep level of involvement of American law enforcement and security agencies in Mexico and placed new limits on their access, causing some American officials and analysts to wonder whether it would be deeply committed to confronting the drug gangs. Michele M. Leonhart, the head of the Drug Enforcement Administration, visited Mexico on Friday, and the leaders of Mexico's army and navy are visiting Washington to forge closer ties.

The arrest will probably give doubters some hope, experts said.

"The success of the effort is likely to help build trust after a period of rocky relations on public security issues," said Andrew Selee, a Mexico scholar at the Woodrow Wilson Center in Washington.

Some analysts said the arrest could lead to further fragmentation of the gangs, which would reduce their ability to threaten state authority but might uncork further waves of violence.

"This takedown will boost Peña Nieto several points in the polls, even as he has spurned talking about violence and the narco war," said George W. Grayson, a professor at the College of William and Mary who has written extensively on the drug gangs. "They fragment into 'cartelitos,' which, while dangerous, do not pose a threat to state security."

Mr. Treviño had been the second in command until the Zetas leader Heriberto Lazcano Lazcano was killed in a battle with Mexican marines in October.

His body was carted off by armed men from a funeral home shortly afterward in an episode that turned triumph into embarrassment for Mexico's president at the time, Felipe Calderón, whose tenure was marked by the killing or arrest of several cartel leaders except the most elusive: Joaquín Guzmán, known as El Chapo, the leader of the Sinaloa Cartel, considered the largest and most powerful supplier of cocaine to the United States.

At his peak, Mr. Treviño was widely feared and credited with helping to give the Zetas gang its reputation while transforming it from a hit squad to a mushrooming transnational criminal organization.

"He had all of Mexico and a lot of Central America under his tentacles," said Art Fontes, a recently retired F.B.I. agent who was assigned to Mexico until late last year and is now a security consultant. "He was feared everywhere he went."

In one of the organization's bolder moves across the border, Mr. Treviño used a brother in the United States to launder tens of millions of dollars in drug proceeds by buying and selling expensive American quarter horses. José Treviño, the kingpin's older brother, was convicted this year of running the business, whose operations were first reported by The New York Times.

But a number of drug war analysts have said that Mr. Guzmán's cartel, an older, more established organization less prone to shocking violence, was beginning to overtake the Zetas, the younger, less disciplined outfit that branched out more into extortion, kidnapping and migrant smuggling.

Mexican law enforcement has arrested some of the Zetas' most important leaders, including several of them just before Mr. Calderón's term ended in December.

Insight Crime, a news and analysis Web site that closely tracks drug crime in the Americas, has reported that a Zetas splinter group called Los Legionarios emerged last year "with the express purpose of waging war against Z-40 and his organization."

GINGER THOMPSON contributed reporting from New York.

Arrest of Suspected Drug Lord in Mexico Is Seen as Symbolic Amid Police Scandal

BY DAMIEN CAVE | OCT. 9, 2014

MEXICO CITY — Vicente Carrillo Fuentes was the mediocre heir, the authorities said. He never quite gained the fame or authority of his brother, Amado Carrillo Fuentes — the Juárez cartel's late founder and the kingpin famous for both flying cocaine to the United States in jumbo jets and dying during failed plastic surgery in 1997.

Instead, Vicente was vicious. Mr. Carillo Fuentes, who was arrested Thursday by Mexican authorities in the northern city of Torreon, ran the Juárez ring with an eye for killing and a thirst for allies, according to American and Mexican officials who have been pursuing him for 14 years.

His was the era when the battle between the Juárez and Sinaloa cartels made Ciudad Juárez as bloody and violent as a war zone. And yet at this point, with Juárez far more calm, experts said, his arrest was mostly symbolic.

"By 2012, it was clear his forces had lost, and he went into exile," said Steven S. Dudley, a director of InsightCrime.com, a website that tracks and analyzes Latin American crime trends. "Some thought he was even retired."

Thus the timing of his arrest has raised suspicions among some in Mexico. President Enrique Peña Nieto is in the midst of the largest security scandal of his term, with Mexico and the world aghast at the recent discovery of a mass grave with 28 bodies near a town in the state of Guerrero, where 43 students were reported missing after a confrontation with the police in late September.

At a news conference Thursday, Mexico's attorney general announced that more graves and bodies had been found in the area, and that four more people had been arrested, in addition to the 22 police officers already detained.

The Peña Nieto administration is also weathering criticism from human rights advocates over the way it has handled another case from late June, in which 22 people were killed by Mexican soldiers in a small mountain town near a common drug route. Mexican military officials initially claimed the deaths had occurred in a firefight only to later admit that at least some were killed after surrendering.

Security analysts and former intelligence officers — along with American officials — have been arguing for months that these and other episodes clearly show that Mr. Peña Nieto needs to get serious about reforming the criminal justice system and establishing more effective systems of accountability for security forces, after spending the first two years of his presidency emphasizing the improving economy.

The president, though, has stopped far short of an overhaul. Responding to the case of the missing students, Mr. Peña Nieto delivered a four-minute speech on Monday, in which he kept the focus relatively narrow, saying, "We need to find the truth and make sure the law is applied to those responsible for these outrageous, painful and unacceptable acts." At least in part, some experts said, the theatrics around Thursday's arrest — with Mr. Carrillo Fuentes put on display upon arrival at the airport here — seemed aimed at casting security forces in a better light.

"The Mexican federal government is in desperate need of this kind of success, in order to neutralize the effects of all the attention to what happened in Guerrero," said Raúl Benítez Manaut, a researcher at the National Autonomous University in Mexico City who studies criminal groups.

And yet, he and others added, it was a legitimate success. Mr. Carrillo Fuentes has been on the run for more than a decade. "These people should not be allowed to walk free, unpunished, enjoying their drug-related money," Mr. Benítez said.

Alejandro Hope, a former intelligence official under Mexico's last president, Felipe Calderón, added that the positive attention from an arrest dissipates too quickly — and the arrests themselves are too hard to obtain — to believe that this was simply a political ploy.

If anything, he said, the arrest and its promotion "reinforces the sense of continuity between Calderón and Peña, something the Peña people have been trying to run from."

Indeed, Mr. Carrillo Fuentes, 51, was the second suspected kingpin captured over the last two weeks. On Oct. 1, the Mexican Army arrested Héctor Beltrán-Leyva, 49, who the authorities say is the head of the Beltrán-Leyva cartel. He was caught in the colonial city of San Miguel de Allende while eating dinner at a seafood restaurant.

Both men were heirs to their family businesses, and in middle-age, dinosaurs of the trade. Mr. Carrillo Fuentes often used disguises and moved from city to city, authorities said. Mr. Beltrán-Leyva had been presenting himself as a local businessman.

The new generation of criminal leaders, experts note, tends to be less polished, at least as brutal, and more diffuse in their organizational structure — like the gangs that are believed to have colluded with the police in the case of the missing students. That case, many argue, is far too significant and too telling to be brushed aside by an unrelated arrest.

"If the capture had happened in any other given moment, it would have had a much greater effect and impact, a much bigger political gain for Peña Nieto," said Jorge Chabat, a drug and security expert at CIDE, a Mexico City research group. "But it's happening at a moment where all eyes and everyone's attention is on the missing students."

PAULINA VILLEGAS contributed reporting.

As Drug Kingpins Fall in Mexico, Cartels Fracture and Violence Surges

BY WILLIAM NEUMAN | AUG. 12, 2015

CHILAPA, MEXICO — For nearly a week, gun-toting masked men loyal to a local drug gang overran this small city along a key smuggling route. Police officers and soldiers stood by as the gunmen patrolled the streets, searching for rivals and hauling off at least 14 men who have not been seen since.

"They're fighting over the route through Chilapa," said Virgilio Nava, whose 21-year-old son, a truck driver for the family construction supply business, was one of the men seized in May, though he had no apparent links to either gang. "But we're the ones who are affected."

For years, the United States has pushed countries battling powerful drug cartels, like Mexico, to decapitate the groups by killing or arresting their leaders. The pinnacle of that strategy was the capture of Mexico's most powerful trafficker, Joaquín Guzmán Loera, better known as El Chapo, who escaped in spectacular fashion last month from a maximum-security prison.

And while the arrests of kingpins make for splashy headlines, the result has been a fragmenting of the cartels and spikes in violence in places like Chilapa, a city of about 31,000, as smaller groups fight for control. Like a hydra, it seems that each time the government cuts down a cartel, multiple other groups, sometimes even more vicious, spring up to take its place.

"In Mexico, this has been a copy of the American antiterrorism strategy of high-value targets," said Raúl Benítez Manaut, a professor at the National Autonomous University of Mexico who specializes in security issues. "What we have seen with the strategy of high-value targets is that Al Qaeda has been diminished, but a monster appeared called the Islamic State. With the cartels, it has been similar."

A member of a community defense force in Petaquillas, Mexico. The groups have sprung up in Guerrero State as a response to corruption and police inaction in the face of gang violence.

While the large cartels are like monopolies involved in the production, transportation, distribution and sale of drugs, experts say, the smaller groups often lack international reach and control only a portion of the drug supply chain.

They also frequently resort to other criminal activities to boost their income, like kidnapping, car theft, protection rackets and human trafficking. And while the big cartels have the resources to buy off government officials at the national level, the smaller gangs generally focus on the local and state levels, often with disastrous consequences for communities.

That was abundantly clear in a case that stunned the nation last year, when 43 students disappeared in Iguala, a city a short distance from Chilapa.

Government investigators say that the mayor and the police in Iguala were allied with a local drug gang, which murdered the students and burned their bodies. Like here, the disappearances took place amid a fight over territory between local traffickers.

The fracturing of the cartels into smaller gangs requires a very different approach from what is being pursued at the national level, analysts say.

But even after the disappearance of the students made it obvious that fundamental changes were needed, the violence and abductions here in Chilapa have again laid bare the government's inability or unwillingness to come up with an effective response.

"It's as if nothing ever happened, as if there hadn't been any precedent," said José Reveles, an author of books on drug trafficking.

Successive governments have talked about a vast reform of the country's police, but their efforts failed to weed out corruption and create professional security forces. President Enrique Peña Nieto proposed a series of changes last November, including centralizing control of the local police in each state, but that has not been carried out.

All these problems are on agonizing display here in Chilapa.

Residents and government officials say that Chilapa sits astride a route for smuggling marijuana and opium paste that is contested by two gangs. They ascended after the government succeeded in jailing or killing the leaders of the Beltrán Leyva cartel, which had previously dominated the region.

A group known as the Rojos, or Reds, now controls the city, residents and officials said. But the rural towns nearby are controlled by the Ardillos, whose name is derived from the word for squirrel. Residents have openly accused the mayor of ties to the Rojos, which he denies.

Violence between the groups has been accelerating for months. A candidate for mayor was assassinated in May, a few days after a candidate for governor was menaced by heavily armed men manning a roadblock.

It is common for bodies to be found, sometimes beheaded or with signs of torture. Last month, a beheaded body was left with a note:

"Here's your garbage, possums with tails." Two days later, seven bodies were found. One was decapitated, with a message cut into the torso: "Sincerely, Rojos."

Residents say that the gunmen who overran the town on May 9 were led by the Ardillos. The invaders disarmed the local police and began hauling men off.

"They said, 'Bring us the mayor, bring us El Chaparro,' " said Matilde Abarca, 44, referring to the nickname of the head of the Rojos. Ms. Abarca's 25-year-old son, a fruit seller, was grabbed by a group of masked gunmen, beaten and driven off in a pickup truck.

She said that the gunmen said they would return the abducted residents if the townspeople turned over the Rojos leader. At one point, some residents held a protest march, which the gunmen confronted in a tense standoff.

The occupation occurred even though soldiers and elite federal police officers were stationed in Chilapa because of the rising violence. But instead of forcing out the invaders, witnesses said the authorities simply stood by while the masked gunmen seized and intimidated residents, a contention supported by photographs and cellphone videos.

Some say that the authorities held back because the invaders claimed to be a community defense force, like those that have sprung up elsewhere to confront traffickers in the absence of government action.

The government has been criticized for repressing similar community defense groups, and the paralysis in Chilapa showed its lack of a coherent strategy for dealing with them. Other residents viewed the government's passivity as outright complicity with the gangs.

"When they took the people away, there were police and soldiers there, and they did nothing," said Victoria Salmerón, whose brother, a clothing seller, disappeared during the takeover. "It was as if they were on their side." Since the occupation ended on May 14, federal and state police have stayed on hand to keep order, and officials have pledged to investigate the disappearances. But there is virtually no sign of progress.

Family members of missing people in Chilapa, where masked gunmen loyal to a local drug gang abducted at least 14 men.

Aldy Esteban, the administrator for the municipal government, said that no leaders of either gang had been arrested since the May invasion.

"There's clear evidence who took them, but we've had no answer" from the authorities, said Bernardo Carreto, a farmer who watched his three sons be taken away when they arrived in Chilapa to sell a calf. "They're ignoring us. No one's been arrested. Nothing has happened."

The relatives of the 14 missing men meet daily in a restaurant near the tree-shaded town square. A government human rights official said that 10 more men may have disappeared during the takeover, but that the relatives are too scared to come forward.

Many of them cling to the hope that their loved ones may still be alive, perhaps forced to work on poppy or marijuana farms.

"They took them alive and they must return them alive," said Mr.

Carreto, echoing a slogan used by the relatives of the students who disappeared last year.

In that case, the National Human Rights Commission issued a report in July saying that the investigation into the students' disappearance was deeply flawed and that vital leads were not pursued.

José Díaz, 52, a spokesman for the families here in Chilapa, said that about 100 people in the area have disappeared since the middle of last year, including his two brothers and a cousin.

He said his relatives had no connection to the gangs and were kidnapped simply because they were from Chilapa and entered Ardillo territory. Five headless bodies were later found, which he believes included those of his relatives, but he said that the government has not revealed results of DNA testing that could identify the corpses.

René Hernández, a spokesman for the Mexican attorney general's office, said in an email that investigators have withheld some information from residents "to continue moving forward with the identification and location of the criminal groups in order to take definitive action without putting the residents at risk."

Recent government data shows that the national murder rate has been steadily declining since its peak in 2011, which the government cites as evidence that its approach is working.

Despite the decline, many areas of the country continue to be shaken by violence as smaller groups of traffickers battle to fill the vacuum left by the deterioration of the large cartels.

Experts believe that even the powerful Sinaloa cartel, which is run by Mr. Guzmán, will eventually go the way of other large trafficking organizations and break into pieces, even with its leader once again at large.

"For Mexican organized crime, El Chapo is not the future," said Alejandro Hope, a former Mexican intelligence official. "El Chapo is a remnant, a powerful remnant, but a remnant of the past all the same."

Referring to the violence-convulsed state where Chilapa is, he added, "The future is Guerrero."

Mexico, Signaling Shift, Extradites Drug Kingpins to United States

BY AZAM AHMED | SEPT. 30, 2015

MEXICO CITY — The Mexican government extradited several top drug kingpins to the United States on Wednesday, signaling a change of heart after the stunning escape of Joaquín Guzmán Loera this summer from the nation's most secure prison.

Among the 13 people who were extradited are two top drug lords, including an American citizen, Edgar Valdez Villarreal, also known as "La Barbie," as well as others charged with participating in the murders of an American consulate worker and an American immigration and customs agent.

The extradition of the men, many of whom had been imprisoned for years in Mexico, is a change in tactics for the government. Since President Enrique Peña Nieto came to power in 2012, his government has adopted more of an arms-length approach to the United States on security cooperation than the previous government did. This has often meant taking a more assertive stance in matters of sovereignty, which has included a reluctance to cede control of prisoners to the United States.

Indeed, just weeks before Mr. Guzmán's escape from prison, the United States issued a formal request for his extradition. In the immediate aftermath of his escape, as the Mexican government pondered an offer of unconditional help from the Americans, the frustration between the allies grew.

Wednesday's move, however, appeared to be intended to show a warming of relations, and perhaps a fear of more embarrassment if another prisoner escaped.

"Today's extraditions would not have been possible without the close collaboration and productive relationship the Department of Justice enjoys with officials at the highest levels of law enforcement in Mexico," Attorney General Loretta E. Lynch said in a statement.

Among the most colorful and ruthless of those extradited on Wednesday was Mr. Valdez, who grew up the son of a shop owner in Laredo, Tex., before fleeing to Mexico and climbing his way up the cartel ladder. Nicknamed La Barbie for his looks, he is thought to be one of the only American citizens to have risen so high in the Mexican drug world.

During his time as a top lieutenant in the Beltrán-Leyva Cartel, Mr. Valdez was responsible for some of the most grisly violence of the drug war, including beheading rivals and videotaped executions. He oversaw a cadre of gunmen responsible for battling other drug gangs, including the Gulf Cartel, and is credited with dragging violence into the beach town of Acapulco, which he took over.

Mr. Valdez was arrested in 2010 by Mexican authorities and convicted the next year.

In the United States, Mr. Valdez is wanted on drug charges in both Georgia and Louisiana.

Also extradited was Jorge Costilla Sánchez, who was once the leader of the Gulf Cartel and the Zetas gang and responsible as well for violence that has gripped Mexico over the years.

In addition to Mr. Valdez and Mr. Costilla, Mexican authorities also extradited three men wanted in the murder of a United States consulate worker, her husband and the spouse of another consulate worker in Ciudad Juárez, the border city once engulfed in the violence of the drug war. Prosecutors also said that Jose Emanuel Garcia Sota, charged in the 2011 killing of an Immigration and Customs Enforcement agent, Jaime Zapata, was also among those extradited.

PAULINA VILLEGAS contributed reporting.

CHAPTER 3

The Rule of Pablo Escobar

Before the reign of El Chapo, there was Pablo Emilio Escobar Gaviria. His power and influence as a Colombian drug lord allowed him to hold the country hostage throughout the 1980s and 1990s. Bombings, massacres and urban sieges became the norm in Colombia for much of the latter half of the 20th century, due in no small part to Escobar's funding of left-wing paramilitary groups. More than 20 years after his death, Escobar's legacy is still regarded as one of profligate destruction and wanton violence.

Colombia Starts to Feel Side Effects of Drug Trade

BY ALAN RIDING | MAY 20, 1984

BOGOTÁ, COLOMBIA — While he lived, neither Government nor public seemed to support Justice Minister Rodrigo Lara Bonilla in his campaign against Colombia's powerful narcotics rings. Instead he received only daily death threats for his efforts. Yet Mr. Lara's murder three weeks ago appears to have achieved what he had been unable to accomplish during eight months in office; the Government is waging its first full-scale offensive against drugs, and Colombians have suddenly awakened to the damage caused by narcotics to their entire society.

"It was as if we were anesthetized," a newspaper editor said. "There was tacit toleration. People argued that narcotics brought in dollars, they created jobs, they were an American problem and so on. We learned to coexist with the phenomenon." Even the raids on clandestine cocaine laboratories and the arrests that continued last week suggested that the authorities knew all along who was doing what and where. President Belisario Betancur nevertheless repeated his declaration of war against drugs after what he described as the country's "moral vacations." He added: "There will be no going back."

The United States, which receives 90 percent of its cocaine and 60 percent of its marijuana from Colombia, warmly welcomed the change. Two of the 23 drug operators whose extradition was requested by Washington last year have been arrested and the President has signed a five-month-old extradition order for a third dealer, Carlos Lehder Rivas, who reportedly has fled to Peru.

But dismantling the drug empire will not be easy. With estimated annual revenues of $2 billion, it employs thousands of Colombians to grow coca leaf and process coca paste from Bolivia and Peru. It has also invested in legitimate businesses, weakened the judiciary through threats and corruption and has infiltrated politics.

Many Colombians believe the scene was set for confrontation with political leaders when big drug dealers began meddling too openly in public affairs. "They seemed to think they could buy respectability in just 10 years," a businessman said. "In the Italian mafia, it takes one generation. Here they were too brash, too vulgar, too quick."

When the focus of Colombia's drug trade switched from marijuana to cocaine in the late 1970's, greatly increased fortunes were at first invested in luxury homes, large farms, private aircraft and imported automobiles, as well as expansion of the narcotics business.

Then, as traffickers learned to launder "hot" money through United States banks, they began laundering their image at home. Some bought soccer teams, two built first-rate zoos, one constructed a bullring. Fabio Ochoa Restrepo, who is now in jail, launched a populist "Medellín Without Slums" program in his home town. Drug operators donated hospitals, schools and churches to communities.

During Colombia's 1982 general election, rumors circulated that drug money had poured into the campaigns of many candidates, sometimes without their knowledge. Pablo Escobar Gaviria, a man said by officials to be the country's largest single dealer, was elected to Congress as an alternate deputy. (He still enjoys parliamentary immunity but has fled the country.) Carlos Lehder, who has been indicted on drug charges in the United States, founded a provincial newspaper and the extreme-rightist Latino National Party, which fought against applying the 1982 extradition treaty with the United States. He led demonstrations outside Congress to demand its revocation.

FACING THE CONSEQUENCES

But it was only after an ABC Television special, "The Cocaine Cartel," named Colombia's top three dealers last August that Mr. Ochoa, Mr. Escobar and Mr. Lehder were publicly linked to narcotics in Bogotá. Even after the murder in February of a young lawyer, Edgar Gonzalez, who had challenged the President for not applying the extradition treaty, there was no public outcry. Mr. Lara, the Justice Minister, was almost alone in denouncing "hot" money in politics, in pressing for application of the extradition treaty and working with United States drug enforcement authorities. But since his death, he has been proclaimed a national hero.

The country must still face the consequences of previous indifference. When oversupply drove down the price of pure cocaine, dealers began dumping cocaine base in Colombia and tens of thousands of youths became addicted to what is known here as "bazuka."

Such is the fear and corruption among Colombian judges that the Government declared a state of siege so that dealers could be tried by military tribunals. It was a difficult move for Mr. Betancur. He is the first President in decades to govern without resorting to emergency powers. And success in the crackdown could mean the loss of hundreds of million of dollars in foreign exchange earnings and the likely "flight" of drug money invested in local banks and businesses. Last week officials attributed the sharp rise in the black market price of the dollar to purchases by nervous traffickers.

With their eyes on the past, many Colombians remain skeptical that the Government can keep up its offensive. Some believe that Mr. Lara's murder was ordered by middle-level operators anxious to provoke reprisals against the big-name traffickers. Others argue that the industry will survive so long as demand exists in the United States.

But a former President, Carlos Lleras Restrepo, said Mr. Lara's death had brought the rebirth of morality in Colombia. "It is vital to stimulate and sustain this reaction," he said, "but this depends only partly on actions of the authorities and to a much greater extent on the social conscience."

Cocaine Billionaires: The Men Who Hold Colombia Hostage

BY ALAN RIDING | MARCH 8, 1987

CARLOS LEHDER RIVAS thought he was safe from arrest. In fact, in all of Colombia, there were probably only a handful of officials who believed that he or any of a half-dozen other billionaire cocaine traffickers could be reached by the law. After all, the "mafiosos," as they are known locally, had repeatedly defied the Government, murdering anyone, from Cabinet Ministers to Supreme Court justices, who stood in their way. Through terror and corruption, they had become in many ways more powerful than the state.

It was, therefore, a shock when Lehder, a handsome and arrogant 39-year-old, was arrested, along with 14 bodyguards, at one of his homes on Feb. 4. Within hours, he was on board a United States Government plane en route to Florida to face a long list of drug-related charges. For the first time in a decade of booming cocaine exports, the head of one of the three biggest Colombian dope "families" had been forcibly retired.

But Lehder's deportation also sent shudders of fear throughout Colombia. In recent weeks, the country's leaders have belatedly awoken to certain hard truths: that their country has been taken hostage by organized crime; that they can no longer dismiss the drug problem as one created exclusively by American demand, and that Colombia has developed its own drug-abuse problem. Lehder's arrest suggested that Colombia could fight back. But its strength of will has yet to be tested. Although Lehder is gone, there are other mafiosos, just as ambitious and violent and almost as rich, according to narcotics experts, waiting to take his place.

"Narcotics traffickers are becoming a super-state because of their enormous wealth," Attorney General Carlos Mauro Hoyos noted recently, "But if we allow ourselves to be intimidated by fear or by the power of these people, our future will be more and more uncertain."

For William Jaramillo Gomez, "This is the worst crisis in our entire history because it is a crisis of values." A courageously outspoken politician, Jaramillo knows the problem first-hand, as Mayor of Medellín, the world capital of the cocaine empire and a city so dangerous that the United States Drug Enforcement Administration has long since closed its office there. "When I speak out," the Mayor continues, "I feel moral and intellectual support but I hear silence because there is fear."

Colombian President Virgilio Barco Vargas, who assumed office last August, had given little priority to fighting the narcotics problem until late in December, when an upsurge in drug-related violence forced him to act. The offensive he launched then brought mediocre results until the capture of Lehder. But Lehder's extradition on charges of drug trafficking is likely to bring reprisals from drug-world kingpins unaccustomed to being challenged.

One prominent newspaper editor, who would speak only from behind a shield of anonymity, cannot shake off his pessimism. "We have grown used to living by the law of the jungle," he says. "I have no confidence that in the end good shall triumph over evil."

AS COLOMBIA SLIPS EVER deeper into what one Government official has called "the devil's caldron," its leaders admit they have no real solutions.

The very weapons needed to fight the war against drugs have been virtually neutralized by violence or bribery. The police and armed forces, either through fear or because they have been paid off, fail to move against major traffickers, even when their whereabouts are known. (Carlos Lehder was apprehended only after Medellín's top police commanders had been replaced a few days before the event.) Congress, packed with politicians whose election campaigns were financed by drug money, is silent on the issue. Some prominent members of the traditional Liberal and Conservative parties are known to be tied into the cocaine cartel, but leftist guerrilla groups have also found arguments to justify taking drug money. The courts have been paralyzed by the succession of judges — 57 at the last count — who have been murdered for refusing payoffs or for ignoring the threats of drug operators. Even the Roman Catholic Church, which until three years ago accepted charitable donations from drug bosses in search of respectability, has had surprisingly little to say on the subject.

Above all, there is fear: those who in any manner dare to combat narcotics traffickers live under the constant threat of death. The United States Embassy in Bogotá is a bunker, with many diplomats going around armed. President Barco's predecessor, Belisario Betancur, who angered the drug mafia by launching an antidope campaign, is protected by some 40 Government bodyguards. Others have discovered that there is no safe haven, even abroad. Former Justice Minister Enrique Parejo Gonzalez, for example, took up the post of Ambassador to Hungary and, on Jan. 13, miraculously survived an assassination attempt outside his residence in Budapest. The drug bosses had made their point: they could even break through the Iron Curtain. Revenge also eventually caught up with Col. Jaime Ramirez, a respected former antinarcotics police chief, who was assassinated last November, 11 months after he had resigned from office.

Prominent among the few Colombians who have publicly denounced the cocaine "capos" have been journalists. In reprisal, 24 have been killed over the past three years. Guillermo Cano Isaza, editor and publisher of El Espectador, Bogotá's second-largest newspaper, wrote that "it is as if the public were itself drugged, unable to see that the power of narcotics traffickers is growing in a colossal way." As he drove alone and unarmed on Dec. 17, he was murdered by two gunmen riding on a red motorcyle. His death shocked the country's elite.

COCAINE HAD LONG BEEN AROUND — it was even fashionable in aristocratic circles in Victorian England — but the special "talent" of Colombia's new mafiosos was to convert cocaine into a mass-market drug, cheap enough for students and secretaries, "safe" enough for bankers and businessmen. In a remarkably short time, they had seized control of the entire operation, from the purchase of coca leaves and paste from poor farmers in Peru and Bolivia, through the processing of pure cocaine hydrochloride in Colombian laboratories and up to the final retail distribution in the United States. (An estimated 80 tons a year now go to the United States.)

Pablo Escobar Gaviria, who tops the world's most-wanted list of cocaine traffickers, is referred to reverently by the people of Medellín as Don Pablo, which seems reasonable for someone said to be worth more than $2 billion. Then there are the Ochoas, also of Medellín: Don Fabio, the father, and his sons Fabio, Juan David and Jorge Luis, whose involvement in cocaine has pushed them into the billionaire class. Carlos Lehder Rivas, who is now awaiting trial in Florida, completes the high command of the so-called Medellín cartel, although he comes from the city of Armenia, 100 miles to the south. Since 1978, this cartel has smuggled an estimated $10 billion worth of pure cocaine into the United States.

Why Medellín? First, its strategic location in northwest Colombia and excellent air connections. Then too, the outstandingly good cover provided for clandestine cocaine laboratories by the rolling hills that surround it. The town's industrial tradition guarantees the availability of chemicals needed for cocaine processing. Finally, a slump in its crucial textile sector in the 1970's thrust onto the streets thousands of young men, many of whom became "mules" or "guns" for the traffickers.

As their empire expanded, the new capos were at first predictable, covering their flanks by paying off local police and politicos and exhibiting their new wealth in cars, aircraft and fine horses, as well as haciendas and mansions. But their real dream was to buy respectability, to be accepted in traditional social circles. And, perhaps to their surprise, Medellín society was delighted to enjoy their wealth without publicly questioning its source.

"Soon the narcos were even seen working out their deals inside the Union Club and the Country Club," one local businessman recalls. "They were being accepted. It was amazing."

So blatant was the penetration that the descriptive "narco" was soon attached to anyone thought to be influenced in any manner by the capos: narco-guerrillas, narco-journalists, narco-judges, narco-politicians, and so on.

The Ochoas, Escobar and Lehder were only the biggest operators. There were others, like Gonzalo Rodriguez Gacha and Gilberto Rodriguez Orjuela, whose brother, Miguel, bought the America soccer team as well as the Grupo Radial Colombiano radio network. But the greater wealth and power of the big three families of Medellín pushed them into the limelight. For a while, they seemed content. The Ochoas sponsored bullfights and rarely missed a horse show. Lehder's principal eccentricity, beyond an open admiration for Adolph Hitler, was to commission a statue of a bullet-riddled John Lennon for display at a luxurious country-style hotel he built.

Escobar, whose pride was a zoo he built at Puerto Triunfo, was the first to see the wisdom of becoming a social benefactor. He contributed money to church-run charities, which accepted it, Bishop Dario Castrillon of Pereira later explained, "to prevent it from being invested in brothels, the production of drugs or any other crime." Escobar also established a program called Medellín Without Slums, which, under the administration of a Roman Catholic priest, built some 500 small houses for squatters on a hillside overlooking the city.

The investment was not wasted. His image as "Don Pablo the Good" won Escobar election in 1982 as an alternate Congressman for Antioquia province on the ticket of a faction of the Liberal Party.

THE TRAFFICKERS HAD GOOD reason to become involved in politics. An extradition treaty in 1979 made it possible for the first time for them to be sent for trial to the United States. The prospect of spending decades in an American jail was unappealing. In response, they financed a propaganda blitz in Colombia's newspapers and in its Congress. Lehder even founded his own daily, Quindio Libre, and formed the Latino National Party to help stir nationalist indignation over the idea of Colombians being tried by a foreign court. The propaganda suggested that everyone in Colombia was somehow benefiting from the "narco-dollars" entering the country. The message seemed to get through. Four years later, although American requests piled up, President Betancur had not signed a single extradition order.

Then, in the fall of 1983, Rodrigo Lara Bonilla, the newly appointed Justice Minister, ordered the arrest of "extraditable" drug traffickers. The capos felt threatened. The following April, after Colombian and American agents had raided a jungle laboratory and seized an unprecedented 27,500 pounds of pure cocaine, with a street value of some $1.2 billion, Lara was murdered as he drove home at dusk by a gunman riding on the back of a motorcycle.

This time, the public reacted with indignation. Echoing the emotions of the moment, President Betancur declared "a war without armistice" against narcotics traffickers and promptly signed the pending extradition order for Carlos Lehder, though it would be almost three years before it was executed.

In the year that followed, President Betancur and his new Justice Minister, Enrique Parejo, approved the extradition of 12 Colombians and a German to the United States, while three Americans and a Colombian were extradited back to Colombia. For the first time in years, Washington began publicly commending the Colombian Government's antinarcotics efforts, and while none of the peces gordos (the big fish) were caught, major traffickers were forced into hiding.

The top traffickers made a peace gesture, an almost-impudent invitation for President Betancur to "consider our reincorporation, in the near future, into Colombian society." In exchange for the extradition treaty not being applied retroactively, they offered to withdraw from the narcotics business, pull out of politics and repatriate their capital, said to be hidden in accounts in the United States, Panama and Western Europe. (A less formal offer two years later suggested they would also pay off Colombia's $13 billion foreign debt.)

Still more astonishing, a former President of Colombia, Alfonso Lopez Michelsen, was willing to discuss the offer with Pablo Escobar and Jorge Luis Ochoa at a secret meeting in Panama, where the capos had fled. The Attorney General, Carlos Jimenez Gomez, then flew to Panama to receive the traffickers' offer at another clandestine meeting. Neither politician informed American authorities of the whereabouts of the two fugitive capos.

In reality, it was not long before the traffickers were back in Medellín. Word would reach Bogotá that Escobar had been out drinking at the local Hilton, or that the Ochoas had been seen at a horse show, but they were always accompanied by private armies of thugs carrying barely concealed submachine guns.

Even when caught, the big fish were slippery. Within weeks of being extradited from Spain, Jorge Luis Ochoa managed to be freed on bail and vanished. Then there was Juan Ramon Matta Ballesteros, a Honduran who served as middleman between Colombian and Mexican traffickers. One Sunday afternoon in March 1985, he distributed $2 million among prison guards in Bogotá and walked out to freedom.

But the traffickers continued to fear extradition. In November 1985, guerrillas from the April 19 Movement, or M-19, seized the Palace of Justice in downtown Bogotá and, according to American officials, promptly destroyed all documents related to pending extraditions as part of a "contract" with drug bosses. As the Army counterattacked, 11 of the nation's 24 Supreme Court justices were among those killed.

Over the last five years, of the 57 judges killed, 36 were from lower courts. Although election to the Supreme Court had always been an honor, several justices have chosen to resign. In January, the court's president, Fernando Uribe Restrepo, stepped down and moved to Ecuador. His temporary successor, Nemesio Camacho Rodriguez, said at the time, "We're all intimidated, but I don't feel fear." Five days later, he, too, resigned.

PERCHED ON THE MUDDY banks of a river that cuts through Colombia's lowlands, San Jose del Guaviare is a monument to the insatiable world demand for cocaine. Starting in the early 1980's, poor migrants flocked to the region to cut down trees, plant coca and then transform its bright-green leaves into a brown powdery substance called coca base. No traditional crop was so remunerative. And San Jose, where growers made their sales, spent their money and sorted out their differences, reflects this boom. It has grown tenfold, to 24,000 inhabitants, and its streets have sprouted bars, brothels and nightclubs. A new airport terminal is under construction. Violence is rampant, although last year "only" 82 murders were recorded, down from 150 in 1985.

Some 180 antinarcotics police and 300 soldiers are stationed in San Jose, but they rarely leave town. The police have suspended raids on the rudimentary laboratories that make coca base until their helicopters are armored. "We kept being shot at," one officer explains. And the Army has virtually stopped patrolling since a truce with the Colombian Revolutionary Forces (FARC, the largest of the country's rebel groups, which controls most of the coca fields in the area) went into effect in May 1984.

One hour by motorboat up the Guayabero River from San Jose is the village of Raudal. The mood there was relaxed on a recent weekend. The numerous bars were crowded with peasants fighting off the heat with chilled beer. Most were coca growers and some were clearly well off: one casually bet the equivalent of $75 on a cockfight. A few men wearing some item of khaki suggested a discreet guerrilla presence. No more seemed necessary. The FARC's authority is accepted and in many ways welcomed for the order it brings.

The United States has used the "FARC-narc" connection to support its claim that leftists and traffickers are in league. It has also charged that other guerrilla groups, notably the M-19, have connections with drug rings, at times obtaining weapons or levying "taxes" in exchange for allowing drug operations in areas they dominate.

Yet the "FARC-narc" connection is more complex. FARC rebels in the Guaviare region are known to receive income from intermediaries who buy coca base, but they say they "allow" cultivation of coca because peasant farmers cannot subsist with ordinary crops. And since they seem intent on establishing a stable social base in the area, they impose rules to protect the farmers. They fix the maximum day rate that transient pickers can charge; and to protect the community, they impose severe penalties — including death, it is said — on those who consume or push drugs.

The farmers, however, now want to get out of coca. For some years, they had found it profitable to grow a lower-quality tropical version of the plant because coca producers in Peru and Bolivia seemed unable to keep up with demand. And even after falling cocaine prices in the United States in 1983 signaled overproduction, drug operators were able to dump surplus coca base into Colombian cities.

When smoked with tobacco, the base, known as bazuco, produces an instant high and a strong craving. Within a couple of years, its consumption became so widespread that, for the first time, Colombia faced a major abuse problem of its own. Yet overproduction continued. When the local price of a kilogram of coca base dropped to less than one-fifth of what it was five years ago, farmers in the Guaviare area began looking for alternative crops. The FARC spotted the problem and seized the initiative.

Last Dec. 21, mobilized by the guerrillas, some 23,000 peasants arrived in canoes to occupy San Jose as a way of pressuring the Government to invest in the region. "People would prefer to grow corn, yucca, cacao or bananas, but they don't get a decent price," explained Jorge Solano, a local leader of the Patriotic Union, a party set up by the FARC and the Communist Party after their 1984 truce.

The action brought results. Although not mentioned in the final agreement worked out with officials, it was understood that coca cultivation would be phased out if the Government improved roads, built schools and clinics, provided land titles and facilitated the marketing of new products.

LAST DEC. 14, THE SUPREME COURT ruled the extradition treaty to be unconstitutional on technical grounds. President Barco was able to sign it back into effect. The assassination of Guillermo Cano, the newspaper publisher, came three days later. Picking up the challenge, the President invoked emergency powers to involve both the Army and police in a new offensive, and military tribunals were ordered to handle key narcotics cases. The shooting of Ambassador Parejo in Budapest then signaled a new escalation. Now, with the capture and extradition of Carlos Lehder, the Government has thrown down its most serious challenge to date.

Yet the wealth and violent power of the drug empire remains intact, while judges still live in terror and threats against journalists escalate. "For the first time in my life, I'm driving a bullet-proof car," says Hernando Santos, publisher of El Tiempo, the country's largest daily, "but I know that precautions are useless."

Even the capture of a "big fish" assures no respite because dozens of second-level traffickers are reportedly waiting to take over. "We've even heard that they ordered Cano's murder in the knowledge the big capos would take the heat," one foreign narcotics expert said. (Narcotics experts say that when murders involve prominent individuals the big capos are each required to contribute to the fee of the paid assassin, in order to insure shared responsibility.)

Yet perhaps most undermining of the Government's campaign is the growing mood of resentment over the price Colombia is paying for fighting its war against drugs. Increasingly, Colombians feel their country has been taken hostage by a mafia created, sustained and financed by the demand for drugs in the United States, a demand that the United States is doing too little to combat. When the Reagan Administration recently slashed its 1988 budget for domestic antinarcotics programs, this was headline news in a country that has often been urged by official American visitors to do more.

In many political and intellectual circles, the old argument that Colombia is "poisoning" the United States with drugs is now frequently reversed. And in this atmosphere of controversy, even Lehder's extradition was not unanimously applauded.

The idea of legalizing narcotics as a way of dismantling the cocaine mafia is in itself not new, but it was significant that it should be proposed last December by a prominent jurist, Samuel Buitrago Hurtado, president of a senior administrative tribunal known as the Council of State. "This is a personal view," Buitrago said in a television interview, "but I think we're being 'useful fools' in this conflict by paying an immense social cost without obtaining any benefit in return." The suggestion was officially dismissed as "absurd," yet it has since gained new respectability.

In January, no less a stir was caused by Alvaro Gomez Hurtado, the defeated Conservative candidate in last year's Presidential elections, who charged there was "moral imbalance" in the way the problem was viewed.

"We are not aware," Gomez wrote acidly, "that Colombian authorities have protested the American democratic system's notorious and demoralizing tolerance for consumption and traffic of drugs in its own territory."

Yet Colombia remains trapped. While an increasingly heated debate accompanies its Government's offensive, the country is caught in a war that it must pay an enormous price to win and will pay a still higher price if it loses. If victorious, society and state should gradually recover control over Colombia's institutions. But in the process, more officials, police, judges and journalists will inevitably die. The price of defeat, on the other hand, is for the country's political, social and moral supports to be totally undermined by violence and corruption. More than ever, Colombia is now fighting for its own survival.

ALAN RIDING is The Times's bureau chief in Rio de Janerio.

Surrender in Colombia

EDITORIAL | **BY THE NEW YORK TIMES** | JUNE 22, 1991

COLOMBIAN OFFICIALS HAIL the surrender of Pablo Escobar, the infamous leader of the Medellín drug cartel, as the beginning of a new era of domestic tranquillity. But celebrations are premature. Colombia's President, Cesar Gaviria Trujillo, must first persuade the world that the arrest is more than a momentary triumph — and that he and his Government are truly serious about fighting drugs.

The hunt for Pablo Escobar began in earnest in 1989 after the assassination of a presidential candidate, Luis Carlos Galan. Colombian authorities pressed a campaign against drug traffickers, destroying their laboratories, seizing their property and arresting those they could find. But top leaders like Pablo Escobar avoided capture.

When Mr. Gaviria took office last year, he announced a new policy. If traffickers agreed to surrender and confess to a crime, Colombia would spare them what they feared the most: extradition to the United States. Instead, Colombia would strengthen its judiciary and prosecute the drug barons at home. A number of traffickers responded, culminating in the Escobar surrender this week.

His decision apparently reflects his fear that the police would kill him on the spot. He also faced additional threats from rival cartels and guerrilla groups he once considered allies.

As a result, he insisted that he be confined to special quarters where the security measures are designed as much to keep assassins out as to keep him in.

Colombia's willingness to negotiate such matters properly raises questions: How effective is the new Colombian judiciary and can it prosecute Mr. Escobar seriously? Will he be sentenced to more than a token term? Will he be prevented from conducting business from

Pablo Escobar in February 1988.

prison? And will the authorities move to strip him of the assets — land, money, airplanes — that sustain his power?

Without reassuring answers, Pablo Escobar's surrender of freedom may end in Mr. Gaviria's surrender of credibility.

Jailed Drug Cartel Chief
Still Feared in Colombia

BY JAMES BROOKE | JAN. 21, 1992

ENVIGADO, COLOMBIA — Seven months after Pablo Escobar, Colombia's most notorious drug trafficker, entered a luxury jail here, his word still inspires terror across the land.

One recent morning, Ariel Otero, a prominent leader of rightist death squads that killed suspected leftists, told reporters that Mr. Escobar, a former ally, had put out a contract on his life. In revenge, Mr. Otero said he planned to give the police documents and cass-ette tapes implicating the Medellín cocaine trafficker in a series of murders.

Within hours, Mr. Otero was kidnapped. Two days later, his body was found, severely disfigured by torture but easily identifiable by a sign reading: "Ariel Otero: Traitor."

PAPER OMITS CHARGES

But when Medellín's largest selling newspaper, El Colombiano, reported the killing, editors chose to omit Mr. Otero's accusations against Medellín's most powerful native son.

Mr. Escobar's power could also be seen after the Army officer who supervised construction of the jail here told all in memoirs published last month.

Fearing retribution by his former prisoner, Augusto Bahamon Dussan, a retired colonel, now waits in the safety of an Army base until emigration procedures can be completed.

In a series of revelations that have intrigued Colombians, Mr. Bahamon wrote that the trafficker ordered the jail built on his own land and according to his own specifications.

"Escobar not only bought the farm where the jail was to be built, but also 11 more farms around it in order to free himself of curious neighbors and to completely dominate the mountain ridge," Mr. Bahamon wrote in "My War in Medellín."

Mr. Bahamon, an engineer by training, wrote that the mountainside jail here included five elements that are "trademarks" of the trafficker's rural headquarters: "Excellent observation advantage of the surroundings, a soccer field, a natural waterfall for bathing after sports, a lagoon and one electric fence parallel to another to allow a run for guard dogs."

"Pablo Escobar intervened down to the smallest details," wrote the colonel, who retired one month after Mr. Escobar entered the completed jail complex last June 19.

In contrast, Colombia's president, Cesar Gaviria Trujillo, wrote in an Op-Ed page article in The Washington Post one week after Mr. Escobar surrendered that the jail here "is a place designed specifically to hold dangerous criminals."

According to the retired colonel, there are more criminals at the jail than Mr. Escobar and his 17 confederates, who surrendered in return for reduced sentences and immunity from extradition to the United States.

Of 20 jail guards assigned by Envigado's Mayor, an "unconditional" ally of Mr. Escobar, Mr. Bahamon wrote, "Eleven had criminal records."

In a series of responses to written questions and statements faxed to Colombia news organizations, Mr. Escobar has said that he no longer deals in cocaine and that he was not the author of threats against Mr. Otero last week. The statements are accompanied by the trafficker's signature and a thumb print.

Since he entered the jail, he has refused to be photographed by the police, a standard procedure for detainees here. No policeman has dared to press the issue.

Little is known about Mr. Escobar's jail routine other than that he spends much of his time giving sworn depositions to the investigating judge. Under the Government's clemency deal, Mr. Escobar has agreed to plead guilty to one count of trafficking cocaine to the United States.

PROTECTING THE JUDGE

To keep the judge's identity secret, the judge listens to testimony from behind a one-way mirror and speaks into an electronic voice distorting device that makes it impossible to tell if the judge is male or female. For further protection, the judge arrives hooded in a Jeep up the winding road to Mr. Escobar's jail.

Apparently convinced that the United States will attempt an air raid on the jail, Mr. Escobar persuaded Colombian authorities to close the air space over the jail. One month after the trafficker was incarcerated here, an airplane contracted by the State Department for anti-drug work made an emergency landing at Medellín's International Airport.

Colombian authorities said that Colombian soldiers guarding the jail fired on the plane, damaging a motor. State Department officials have declined to say more than that the plane developed "engine trouble."

Skeptical that a Colombian jury will convict Mr. Escobar, American officials are reluctant to send evidence to Colombia. Under American and Colombian law, it is rare that a person can be tried twice for the same crime.

OFFICIAL TO VISIT U.S.

On Jan. 20, Colombia's Justice Minister, Fernando Carrillo Florez, is to travel to Washington in an effort to bring home evidence for a trial this year of Mr. Escobar.

"In this country, no one will dare to testify," said Enrique Parejo Gonzalez, a former justice minister who survived a Medellín cartel assassination attempt in 1987. "Any witness against Pablo Escobar is a dead man."

Virtually the only voice left in Colombia to attack the drug cartels openly, Mr. Parejo described the hilltop jail here in a December radio interview as Mr. Escobar's "general headquarters."

One day recently, Mr. Parejo could be found secluded in a curtained apartment in Bogotá, protected by 24-hour armed guard. "I've heard that the head of the Medellín cartel has ordered my death," the former justice minister said, referring to Colombia's most powerful prisoner.

Escobar Suggests He May Surrender

SPECIAL TO THE NEW YORK TIMES | SEPT. 9, 1992

BOGOTÁ, COLOMBIA, SEPT. 8 — Pablo Escobar, the fugitive Colombian cocaine lord who escaped in July from a luxurious prison, has said he will consider surrendering, but warned that any attempt by the United States to abduct him would bring grave consequences.

In remarks published today in the newspaper El Nuevo Siglo, the Medellín cartel boss said he might turn himself in if the Government insured his safety and provided a jail in his home state of Antioquia.

Mr. Escobar gave himself up in June 1991, but after his escape six weeks ago an embarrassed President Cesar Gaviria declared that any new surrender would have to be unconditional.

El Nuevo Siglo said it sent questions to Mr. Escobar — it did not indicate how — and received his replies in the mail. To guarantee the authenticity of his replies, Mr. Escobar included his thumb print and a cassette recording of his voice.

A WARNING TO THE U.S.

Asked about the possibility of being captured by the United States, Mr. Escobar said, "The United States could expose itself to the kidnapping of its own citizens who could be exchanged for those abducted" by American agents.

Mr. Escobar and nine of his lieutenants walked past hundreds of army soldiers on July 22 during a failed Government attempt to transfer them to a military camp.

Since then Mr. Escobar has evaded a huge manhunt mounted by the Government, probably by hiding out in a network of safe houses he has cultivated over the years.

The United States is conducting surveillance flights over Antioquia in an attempt to find Mr. Escobar, who has been indicted in several United States courts on charges of terrorism, murder and cocaine trafficking.

The Bush Administration has also added $2 million to the $1.4 million bounty the Colombian Government has put on Mr. Escobar's head.

Mr. Escobar told El Nuevo Sieglo that he would accept a less luxurious jail than the one from which he escaped in the mountains surrounding his hometown of Envigado.

The inmates had their own Jacuzzis, wet bars, wide-screen televisions, cellular phones, computers, fax machines and even weapons.

Officials say that during his yearlong stay in Envigado, Mr. Escobar put up photos of himself dressed as Pancho Villa and Al Capone and gave parties where prison guards served as waiters. He also continued running his multibillion-dollar drug empire from jail, ordering killings and holding kangaroo trials in which he sentenced cartel rivals to death, officials said.

'MODEST' JAIL NEEDED

Mr. Escobar said that he was not sure if he would surrender again but that his lawyers had contacted the General Prosecutor's office to negotiate a possible sentence.

He said he would need "a very humble and modest jail in Antioquia, but with the absolute guarantee that I would not be transferred for any reason and with the same guarantees that every Colombian prisoner has."

In an interview with the Caracol radio network today, the General Prosecutor, Gustavo de Greiff, insisted that he was not negotiating with Mr. Escobar's lawyers. But he said incarceration in Antioquia was a possibility because all Colombian prisoners had the right to be jailed near their families.

President Gaviria came under fire for his 1991 deal with Mr. Escobar and other Medellín cartel leaders, which offered them special jails and reduced sentences in exchange for surrendering.

Mr. Escobar, whom the police accuse of murdering thousands, says he believes he must remain in Antioquia if he is to avoid being killed by enemies who include the police, the families of people he supposedly killed, the United States and rival drug traffickers.

Old Drug Allies Terrorizing Escobar

BY JAMES BROOKE | MARCH 4, 1993

BOGOTÁ, COLOMBIA, MARCH 3 — Pablo Escobar Gaviria, a veteran practitioner of terrorism, is suddenly squirming as a target of terrorism.

In a modern gang war complete with faxed communiques and clandestine news conferences, a powerful faction of the Medellín cocaine cartel has turned on its godfather and vowed his destruction.

"May Pablo Escobar disappear from the face of the earth," a hooded member of Colombia Libre recently told Semana, a news weekly here. Free Colombia is the civilian wing of a paramilitary Medellín terrorist group known as Pepes, the Spanish acronym for People Persecuted by Pablo Escobar.

Free of scruples about using terror and armed with inside information acquired during years of service for Mr. Escobar, these groups appear to be turning the tables in the seven-month-old manhunt for the nation's most-wanted criminal.

"The Pepes can do what the security forces can't do — blow up someone's house, kidnap people and kill them," Defense Minister Rafael Pardo said in an interview. "They are waging a dirty war."

REFUGE SOUGHT FOR FAMILY

Having lost his monopoly on terrorism, the billionaire trafficker sounds more and more like a hunted man.

In faxed answers on Tuesday to questions submitted by The New York Times through his lawyers, Mr. Escobar whittled a long list of surrender conditions down to one: United States residence visas for his family.

Today, the United States Embassy here rejected that option, issuing a statement that his "offer to exchange protection for his family for his surrender is unacceptable." The Colombian prosecutor, Gustavo de

Greiff, told a radio station today that his office would consider protecting Escobar family members if they made a request.

Left largely on his own, Mr. Escobar is discovering that former friends can be the worst enemies.

"Some of the Pepes were close to him," a law enforcement official here said. "Now they are very dangerous to him."

In one month, the Pepes have killed over 20 Escobar loyalists and carried out 11 dynamite attacks, causing damage of about $8 million to properties owned by the Escobar family. Operating in the Medellín area, Pepes squads have burned ranches and chalets of family members, exploded car bombs outside their apartments, and burned the trafficker's prized collection of antique cars, including a 1933 Pontiac supposedly once owned by Al Capone.

FINANCIER IS SLAIN

"We want to make Pablo Escobar feel the effects in his own flesh of his brand of terrorism," the group said in its inaugural communique on Jan. 31. "Every time that Pablo Escobar carries out an act of terrorism against defenseless people, we will respond with a similar act."

On Monday morning, the mutilated body of an Escobar financier, Juan Guillermo Londono White, appeared, identified by a Pepes placard: "Servile frontman and initiator of kidnappings for Pablo Escobar. Pepes."

A few hours later, the dead man's panic-stricken brother, Diego Londono White, surrendered to the police, reportedly bringing with him the numbers of Escobar accounts in banks here and overseas.

Last week, in a public warning that no political ally of Mr. Escobar was safe, a Pepes gunman sprayed automatic weapon's fire into the offices of a friendly mayor, leaving behind a message: "Watch out politicians servile to Pablo Escobar. Pepes."

"In a few weeks, the Pepes have given the impression of having weakened Escobar more than the Government has in many years," Enrique Santos Calderon, an influential newspaper columnist, wrote on Sunday.

But despite public euphoria over the blows delivered to the Escobar gang, many people here warn that this war could give birth to a new trafficking cartel.

"It's a very dangerous situation," a diplomat here said today. "What you could be seeing is the creation of a new Medellín cartel."

The core of Pepes appears to be composed of survivors of the Galeano and Moncada gang families. Last June, in a dispute over $20 million in stolen drug proceeds, about 15 associates of these families were summoned to Mr. Escobar's jail in Envigado, a Medellín suburb. After a violent argument, Mr. Escobar ordered a purge that reportedly took the lives of 50 members of the two groups.

After escaping from the jail on July 22, Mr. Escobar made additional enemies by kidnapping allies to force payment of tribute to maintain his war against the Colombian Government.

"A lot of people who were kidnapped and blackmailed by Escobar are supporting the Pepes," Fernando Brito, the director of Colombia's Investigative Police, said today.

Publicly, Mr. Escobar refuses to acknowledge that his worst enemies are former allies. Instead, he charges that Pepes is backed by his historic enemies: the rival Cali cocaine cartel and the Medellín police force.

Escobar Offers to Yield
and Colombia Likes Terms

SPECIAL TO THE NEW YORK TIMES | MARCH 18, 1993

BOGOTÁ, COLOMBIA, MARCH 17 — The fugitive drug trafficker Pablo Escobar has proposed a new set of conditions for his surrender, and Colombia's chief prosecutor said today that they were acceptable.

In a message delivered to the Roman Catholic Bishop of the city of Bucaramanga by one of Mr. Escobar's lawyers this morning, the drug trafficker said that to avoid being poisoned he wanted private cooking facilities when in prison. He also asked that he be allowed to call family members three times a week and that they be given Government protection.

Since his escape from prison last July, Mr. Escobar, the head of the Medellín cocaine trafficking ring, has made repeated attempts to negotiate his surrender, but up to now the authorities have refused all of his offers. Two weeks ago, Mr. Escobar said he would turn himself in if the United States Government would protect his family, but Washington refused.

After hearing of Mr. Escobar's latest message, the Chief Prosecutor, Gustavo de Greiff said, "I do not see any difficulty in abiding by these requests, not as a concession but as a solution."

But a senior Government official sought to dampen expectations that Mr. Escobar's offer would make his surrender more likely. "Escobar is like a poker player," he said. "He is testing his cards. But this does not necessarily mean surrender."

The official added that the Colombian Government was not seeking Mr. Escobar's surrender and still intended to capture him. "A surrender is a legal instrument and the decision lies with the criminal," he added.

The drug lord's new proposals are modest compared with the conditions he set for his first surrender in 1991 when, among other concessions, he was allowed his choice of security guards.

A member of a special forces Colombian army unit watches as an army helicopter takes off from a makeshift helicopter landing strip at a small village near Medellín last month. Hundreds of special police and army units have been deployed around Medellín in an effort to locate Pablo Escobar, the most wanted criminal in the Western Hemisphere.

If he were to surrender again, he would be eligible for a plea-bargain and a subsequent sentence reduction. However, the chief prosecutor and the judge who tries his case would have to decide whether the information provided by Mr. Escobar is sufficient to allow for a sentence reduction.

Mr. Escobar is held responsible for much of the violence that has ravaged Colombian cities since the late 1980's. Eighteen indictments are pending against him in Colombia for murder, kidnapping, jailbreak and drug trafficking, and courts in the United States have charged him with conspiracy and drug trafficking.

Since February, the United States and Colombian Governments have been offering a reward of over $6 million for information leading to Mr. Escobar's capture.

Bogotá Drug War Set Back by Court

SPECIAL TO THE NEW YORK TIMES | MAY 5, 1993

BOGOTÁ, COLOMBIA, MAY 4 — The Colombian Government's campaign against drug traffickers has suffered a setback after a high court declared that the chief prosecutor's policy of promising reduced sentences to informers with criminal records was unconstitutional.

There was no official reaction to the decision on Monday, although justice authorities said they would abide by it. Senate President Tito Rueda said Congress would be willing to work with President Cesar Gaviria Trujillo to "work around the vacuum left by the ruling."

With the decision, the authorities have been deprived of a key tool in their fight against the Medellín cartel leader, Pablo Escobar, and other criminal organizations. Deputy chief prosecutor Francisco Sintura admitted as much early today.

President Gaviria had adopted the system of pardons for informers after he declared a state of emergency last November. Since then, security forces and Government officials agree, informers have been the single most effective weapon against Mr. Escobar's organization.

RULING BENEFITS ESCOBAR

The constitutional court, the nation's highest judicial body, ruled that such sentence reductions were tantamount to a pardon and that only politically motivated crimes were eligible for pardon. In any case, the court said, only Congress can approve such measures. While those who have already been promised reduced sentences will not be affected by this decision, the court's ruling may prevent new informers from stepping forward.

The ruling appears to benefit the fugitive Mr. Escobar, who has been in hiding for 10 months now, since escaping last July from Envigado prison, in a Medellín suburb. In addition, it does not affect the Gaviria policy of reduced sentences for criminals who surrender and confess crimes, as could happen in Mr. Escobar's case.

And although most of Mr. Escobar's top henchmen have been captured, killed, or have surrendered to authorities, he has so far evaded a highly trained 1,000-member search team aided by the United States and Britain. Mr. Escobar has also eluded an enemy group that calls itself the Pepes, an acronym in Spanish for People Persecuted by Pablo Escobar, which has wrought destruction on property belonging to the Escobar gang.

This militia announced its disbandment almost two weeks ago, but Mr. Escobar asserted in a letter released Monday that it was still active.

In his message, directed at the chief prosecutor, Mr. Escobar accused the rival Cali drug cartel and the paramilitary chief, Fidel Castano, and his brother of instigating the Pepes. Mr. Escobar added that they periodically tortured and killed union leaders at their headquarters in the city of Medellín. Mr. Escobar, Colombia's most wanted criminal, also accused the authorities of neglecting to go after the Cali cocaine cartel or the Pepes, an assertion the Government has denied.

OFFER TO SURRENDER

As he has done many times before Mr. Escobar offered to surrender in exchange for "public and written guarantees." Mr. Sintura said today that the Government would not negotiate his surrender based on his conditions.

Talks between the Medellín cartel leader and the authorities have reached a virtual standstill. Most of Mr. Escobar's lawyers are believed to have left the country, after the Pepes killed two of them last month and later killed Guido Parra, a mediator between Mr. Escobar and the authorities.

Stripped of many of his top aides, Mr. Escobar has resorted to militia groups and relatively inexperienced hired hands for help, according to members of the security forces. Semana magazine, a national weekly, said he relied on a network of underground bunkers in the Medellín area as his places of refuge.

A Drug Lord Is Buried as a Folk Hero

BY JAMES BROOKE | DEC. 4, 1993

MEDELLÍN, COLOMBIA, DEC. 3 — To chants of "Viva Pablo!" thousands of mourners crowded a muddy hilltop cemetery today to bury Pablo Escobar Gaviria. A ruthless cocaine baron to the outside world, Colombia's most wanted criminal was a folk hero to many poorer residents of Medellín's tough hillside shantytowns.

"He built houses and cared about the poor," lamented a 29-year-old engineering student as mourners scrambled over broken glass in a cemetery chapel window and swarmed around the open casket of the trafficker, who died Thursday in a hail of police bullets. "In the future, people will go to his tomb to pray, the way they would to a saint."

Although a Roman Catholic priest was present, religious ceremonies were forgotten as the raucous mob seized the silver metal coffin and carried it in the pouring rain to the grave site. Fearing for their safety, the traffickers' widow and two children left before the burial.

Jostling to touch the coffin, and sometimes to touch the body, the unruly crowd chanted: "You can feel it! You can feel it! Pablo is present!"

Earlier, during the nightlong wake, a mariachi band defiantly played a popular country ballad, "But I Keep on Being King."

RELIEF AND DELIRIUM

Outside the trafficker's Andean fief here, however, Colombia's mood today was one of rejoicing. "Immortal Joy," proclaimed the headline in La Prensa, Bogotá's main opposition newspaper. "Colombia between relief and delirium."

The Escobar myth grew taller today as more details emerged about his final showdown with the police on a tree-lined suburban street in the Olivos neighborhood here.

The three-story safe house was of the type that allowed Mr. Escobar to evade 15,000 house searches by the police since he escaped from a luxury prison near here 16 months ago. With exits on two different streets, the house also contained a secret chamber under the parquet ground floor.

But worry over the safety of his wife and children apparently led the fugitive to make a false move. Stripped of police protection a week ago, the family unsuccessfully sought asylum in Germany. With an anti-Escobar group already having killed some of the trafficker's more distant relatives, his immediate family took refuge on Monday in a Bogotá hotel.

On Wednesday, his 44th birthday, Mr. Escobar called his family at the hotel on a cellular telephone. He did not know that the United States Drug Enforcement Administration had supplied the Colombian police with electronic monitoring equipment that was programmed to recognize his voice and to locate the source within two minutes.

'WHAT ARE WE TO DO?'

A series of antennas secretly installed last year allowed police technicians to scan all cellular conversations in this bowl-shaped city of two million people, Colombia's second-largest city.

On Thursday afternoon, when two police agents from the elite Search Bloc kicked in the front door of the house here, Mr. Escobar was caught upstairs, in his bare feet.

"Pablo, Pablo, my God, what are we to do?" a young woman could be heard screaming from inside the house.

Cut off from the secret underground hiding place, Mr. Escobar jumped out a window to a rooftop. From there, it would have been a 10-foot jump and a quick sprint to a half-hidden storm sewer ditch that led out of the neighborhood. But the police, who had already cut telephones in the neighborhood, were waiting on all sides.

Alvaro de Jesus Agudelo, an Escobar bodyguard nicknamed The Lemon, started firing to cover his chief's escape attempt. Then Mr. Escobar pulled out two 9-millimeter pistols and started firing from the rooftop.

Police snipers opened up with automatic rifles, hitting Mr. Escobar seven times. When the firing stopped, he lay sprawled on the rooftop, his two guns next to his inert body. The Lemon also lay dead.

Today, as President Cesar Gaviria Trujillo bestowed medals on police officers and agents who carried out the operation, many Colombians braced for reprisals.

Informed of the death on Thursday, Juan Pablo Escobar Henao, the trafficker's 17-year-old son, threatened to personally kill those who had killed his father. He later retracted the death threats, but most Colombians believe that the clan will seek revenge.

"Murderers!" the trafficker's mother, Hermilda Gaviria de Escobar, shrieked at police officers guarding the Medellín city morgue, where the body was taken. Through the same morgue have passed most of Mr. Escobar's murder victims of the last two years, including an estimated 400 policemen.

Bearded, overweight and with a clipped, Hitler-style moustache, Mr. Escobar's body was identified by two sisters and by his parents, who recognized a 10-centimeter gold crucifix implanted in his left shoulder. Fingerprint checks corroborated their identifications.

Warning of more violence, the trafficker's mother said that guerrilla units would try to avenge her son's death. Originally politically motivated, many of Colombia's guerrillas have become hired guns for the nation's $20 billion cocaine industry.

HUNDREDS WAIT IN LINE

Traffic backed up several blocks short of the Montesacro Cemetery in the nearby town of Itagui. By noon, hundreds of people were standing in line waiting to be frisked for handguns before entering the hilltop cemetery.

Rejecting suggestions by local radio announcers that a wake be conducted in the city stadium, the family placed the body on display in a cramped cemetery chapel. But the swelling crowds soon grew

ROBERTO SCHMIDT/AFP/GETTY IMAGES

Hundreds of people waited outside the cemetery where the body of Pablo Escobar Gaviria was to be buried.

impatient. Army guards retreated and people surged forth, breaking through plate glass windows.

"We are 100 percent with Pablo — he fought a lot for the people," Jorge Mario Suarez, a 27-year-old liquor salesman, said as a backhoe dug into the muddy earth to create the final resting place for Colombia's most wanted man.

Pablo Escobar's Home Is Demolished in Colombia, Along With a Painful Legacy

BY MEGAN SPECIA | FEB. 22, 2019

AS THE LOOMING gray building imploded, crumbling into a pile of debris and dust, a crowd of onlookers cheered. Some wept.

The televised blast on Friday that leveled the Monaco building, the former home of the drug kingpin Pablo Escobar in Medellín, Colombia, erased a symbol of the city's past that many have tried to forget. In its place, the city is planning a memorial park to honor the victims of his drug cartel's crimes.

"Today, that building falls and hope begins," President Iván Duque of Colombia said in a televised statement. "It is impossible to change the past, but you can build a better present and a better future."

Mr. Escobar lived in the Monaco building for years until 1988, when rivals bombed it. The Escobar family abandoned the structure, and it has remained vacant ever since. But more than 25 years after Mr. Escobar's death, the six-story building with a penthouse had still caused heated debate, as city officials weighed the potential tourist draw of the site against the urge to move on from a painful past.

The drug lord's legacy has cast a shadow over Medellín, driven in part by new documentaries, television shows like the Netflix hit "Narcos" and books that have focused on Mr. Escobar's life — often neglecting the details of his victims and glorifying his legacy.

In death, he has become something of a folk hero, for his meteoric rise from the working class to billionaire, and for his generosity to some, building houses and hospitals for the poor.

Medellín, called the world's most dangerous city by Time magazine in 1988, has seen violent crime plummet and has increasingly become a tourist destination. Some have capitalized on the city's history as a narcotics hot spot.

Tour guides — including Mr. Escobar's top hit man, John Jairo Velásquez, known as Popeye — take customers on walks through the cartel's old haunts. Street vendors sell T-shirts emblazoned with Mr. Escobar's face.

But the tourist narrative often leaves out the impact of his bloody rise to power and the bribery, kidnappings and killings of anyone who dared defy the cartel.

The mayor of Medellín, Federico Gutiérrez, told the local news outlet El Colombiano ahead of the demolition that knocking down the structure was an important symbolic step forward for the city and the country.

He said that flipping the narrative by emphasizing victims' stories, rather than glorifying the illegal activity of Mr. Escobar and others like him, was essential to reclaiming Colombia's national story.

"We are concerned about the way in which we have narrated, and stopped narrating, our own history," Mr. Gutiérrez said. "In most stories, the perpetrators are the protagonists and this has long-term consequences, because it ends up validating an environment of illegality."

The city consulted with neighbors, academics, local artists and the families of victims to design the memorial park, he said.

The purpose of demolishing the Monaco "is not to erase history," he said. "We need our young people to know the stories, to tell them this cannot happen again."

On Friday, Mr. Gutiérrez joined dozens of victims' families and members of the community for a ceremony on the grounds of a hotel near the Monaco, where they watched the building fall.

"Medellín can tell a different story," he told the crowd. "Today a symbol falls and a light of hope is born."

CHAPTER 4

The Rise and Fall of Frank Lucas

Frank Lucas was born on Sept. 9, 1933, in rural North Carolina. An African-American in the Post-Reconstruction South, Lucas's violent childhood was plagued by institutional racism and hate crimes. Lucas later claimed the murder of a cousin at the hands of the Ku Klux Klan prompted his ultimate relocation to Harlem in the 1960s. Within only a few years, Lucas had established a heroin empire in the New York area. Lucas's dramatic rise and fall are the subject of the 2007 film "American Gangster."

19 Indicted in Heroin Traffic in City

BY JILL GERSTON | JAN. 30, 1975

FEDERAL AND CITY law enforcement officials yesterday announced the indictment of 19 alleged heroin traffickers and the seizure of more than half a million dollars in cash at the home of a couple in Teaneck, N.J.

Frank Lucas, 44 years old, of 933 Sheffield Road, Teaneck, was arrested late Tuesday and his wife, Julia, 28, was held on a conspiracy charge after Federal officials reported seizing $584,683 at their home. The money, in bills of small denominations, was said to have been in five suitcases on a bedroom bureau.

United States Attorney Paul J. Curran and John W. Fallon, director of the New York regional office of the Drug Enforcement Administration, announced the indictments at a news conference at 555 West 57th Street.

5 SEIZED IN BROOKLYN

In a separate incident involving an alleged heroin ring, the police in Brooklyn raided a garage and arrested five men. Accused as head of the ring was Rufus Lee Boyd, 39, owner of Heavy's Racing Enterprises, who, the police said, was arrested in December, 1973, and April, 1971, on similar charges. Also arrested were Mr. Boyd's brothers, James, 31, and William, 37.

Two indictments naming 22 alleged members of an international heroin smuggling ring were unsealed in Federal Court, in Brooklyn yesterday. The indictments named French, Italian, Canadian, Mexican, Argentinian and Urguayan citizens, as well as one naturalized American who is listed as a fugitive.

At the news conference announcing the Teaneck arrest, both Mr. Curran and Mr. Fallon refused to divulge the details that had led to the arrests they said they had resulted from a year-long investigation by agents of the Federal Drug Enforcement Administration and local policemen.

The two officials also refused to comment on whether any of those indicted was connected with the Mafia. Anthony DeLutro, one of those indicted — who is also known as Tony West — is reported to have close links to the Carlo Gambino "family."

$500,000 SALE ALLEGED

According to the indictment, Mr. DeLutro delivered a package containing about 11 pounds of heroin to Anthony Verzino in November, 1973, and received $250,000 in two installments.

In December, 1973, according to the indictment, Mario Perna, named as a co-conspirator, and Ernest Maliza, a defendant, delivered a package containing approximately 22 pounds of heroin to Frank Lucas, a defendant, at the Van Cortlandt Motel in the Bronx.

"These indictments will certainly have an important impact on heroin distribution around the city," said Mr. Fallon. "These people are major organizers who are involved with moving significant amounts of cash and drugs."

If convicted, the 19 defendants could receive maximum penalties of up to 30 years in prison and fines of $50,000 each. Of those indicted, eight persons are already in custody and 11 are still at large, according to the Drug Enforcement Administration.

Mr. Lucas was arraigned yesterday in Federal Court in Manhattan and held in $250,000 bond. His wife, who was not indicted, was also in custody.

In addition the following indicted defendants were in custody:

Joseph Mangano, 43, of 239 N MacQuesten Pkwy., Yonkers.

Anthony DeLutro, 43, of 166 Mulberry St., Manhattan.

Frank Palatta, 42, of 5 Sprain Rd., Hartsdale, N. Y.

Saint Julian Harrison, 51, of 1000 E. 215th St., the Bronx.

Roberto Rivera, 44, of 933 S. Main St., Spring Valley, N. Y.

Frank Caravella, 38, of 411 116th St., Manhattan.

Those indicted but still at large, for whom no addresses were given, were listed as Richard Bolella, Louis Macthiarola, Michael Carbone, Dominic Tufaro, Frank Ferraro, Carmine Margiasso, Anthony Visconti, Joseph Malizia, Ernest Malizia, John Gwynn, William Chapman and Gerard Cachoian.

In Brooklyn, the Boyd brothers — along with Hasty Hyman, 46, and Luther Pipe, 29 — were booked at the 89th Precinct station on 30 charges involving the sale of dangerous drugs. According to the police, the arrests were the result of a six-month investigation by undercover agents who said they had bought 15 "lots" of heroin for $60,000.

The police said that the Boyd brothers were arrested in April, 1971, and December, 1973, on similar charges and were free on bail in that case pending trial. At the time of their 1973 arrest, District Attorney Eugene Gold of Brooklyn estimated their organization's profits "conservatively at $1-million a month."

The Boyds and the two other men are scheduled to be arraigned today in State Supreme Court in Brooklyn.

Lawyer Is Indicted on Perjury Counts For '75 Testimony

BY THE NEW YORK TIMES | JAN. 30, 1977

A PROMINENT NORTH CAROLINA lawyer has been charged in Manhattan with perjury involving his testimony in a 1975 narcotics trial that ended in the acquittal of 13 defendants, including three men who were reputedly among the top narcotics dealers in New York City.

The same trial, which was held in Federal District Court at Foley Square, remains the subject of an investigation into possible jury tampering that reportedly concerned cash payoffs to one or more jurors. Several potential witnesses in the narcotics case were murdered.

The lawyer charged with perjury was identified as John D. McConnell Jr., who is 36 years old and lives in Raleigh, N.C., where he is a partner in the major law firm of Broughton, Broughton, McConnell & Boxley. He is to be arraigned in Manhattan on Feb. 3.

United States Attorney Robert B. Fiske Jr. announced on Wednesday the unsealing of a Federal indictment charging Mr. McConnell with 35 counts of perjury for his testimony in the 1975 trial and for his grand jury testimony in a related narcotics investigation. Mr. McConnell said later that he had no comment on the case.

According to Thomas M. Fortuin and T. Barry Kingham, the prosecutors who presented the perjury case to the grand jury, Mr. McConnell testified in the narcotics trial as a defense witness for Frank Lucas, one of the reputed top narcotics dealers. The prosecutors said the indictment accused Mr. McConnell of lying when he testified in the trial that he had not taken large amounts of cash for Mr. Lucas to banks in the Grand Cayman Islands in the Caribbean. Mr. Lucas was acquitted with the others in the trial, but he was convicted in another narcotics case and is serving a 40-year sentence.

In later grand jury testimony, Mr. McConnell allegedly gave "irreconcilably, inconsistent" testimony that he had received two briefcases containing about $200,000 in cash from Mr. Lucas and had deposited the money in Grand Cayman banks for him.

Mr. McConnell also allegedly told the grand jury that he had been present at least two other times when deposits that he estimated to total as much as $600,000 were made for Mr. Lucas and another narcotics defendant in the banks in the Grand Cayman Islands.

If convicted of the perjury charges, he could face up to five years and a $10,000 fine on each count.

30 Indicted in Queens in Heroin Crackdown

BY MURRAY SCHUMACH | APRIL 5, 1977

THIRTY PERSONS WERE indicted yesterday in what was said to be a $50 million-a-year heroin operation that led from Queens to Asia and back. Among those indicted was a man accused of running the operation from his prison cell.

The crackdown came after more than a year of investigation that ranged from here to North Carolina. The heroin operation reportedly was directed by Frank Lucas, who is serving 70 years on narcotics convictions. Mr. Lucas was said to have considered a plan to have his chief competitor in Harlem, Leroy (Nicky) Barnes, murdered.

The elaborate narcotics operation was described in a 21-page indictment disclosed at a news conference by District Attorney John J. Santucci of Queens. Mr. Lucas and the others were accused in the indictment of conspiring to obtain, possess and distribute heroin in Queens, New York and Bronx Counties.

Sterling Johnson Jr., the citywide special narcotics prosecutor, who played a major role in coordinating the efforts of the Queens, Bronx and Manhattan District Attorney's offices in the investigation, said: "Lucas was the king, but the rest of the operation was loose. There is no evidence that he was accountable to anyone. He gave orders, he did not take orders."

Speaking of the growth of black gangs in narcotics trafficking, Mr. Johnson said: "Organized crime deals with different specialists. But the blacks do it from the womb to the tomb. The blacks cooperate with organized crime and they also compete with it. The blacks are not monolithic."

Mr. Lucas, who is black, is now serving a 40-year sentence in the Federal penitentiary in Lewisburg, Pa., after which he is to serve 30 years on a New Jersey conviction. Much of his direction of the narcotics operation for which he was indicted yesterday allegedly had been done through visitors, giving them directions by a spoken code, while he was in the Essex County Jail in Newark.

Mr. Santucci, who was flanked during the news conference by Mr. Johnson and by Pierre Leval, chief assistant to District Attorney Robert Morgenthau of Manhattan, said he hoped this indictment would lead to others of comparable magnitude.

SOURCE CALLED FAR EAST

Queens became the major base for the operation, in part because a number of defendants lived there and also, Mr. Santucci said, because the suspected criminals believed that a home-owning, middle-class borough would be a better camouflage for major heroin deals than slums such as Harlem or the South Bronx.

Eleven of the 30 defendants lived in Queens. A nightclub, the Show Place Club at 190-03 112 Avenue, Jamaica, Queens, was reported to have been a sort of headquarters for many meetings of the defendants. The club is now closed. Authorities said it had been shut down by the owners after the investigation began.

No explanation was given for the absence in the indictment of any narcotics crimes in Brooklyn. One suggestion, by a person close to Mr. Santucci, was that there was a territorial understanding between this ring and other heroin dealers who had staked out Brooklyn. The bulk of the sales by the defendants were said to be in black areas of the city outside of Brooklyn.

North Carolina figured very importantly in the indictment and in the news conference discussions by the prosecutors. Nearly all those indicted were relatives of Mr. Lucas who had been brought up from North Carolina.

The source of the narcotics was said to be the so-called "Golden Triangle" of Burma, Laos and Cambodia, from which it went to Thailand and then to North Carolina. Mr. Santucci, in answer to questions, said that the area in the vicinity of Fort Bragg in North Carolina was the receiving point for most of the narcotics before being shipped to New York City via New Jersey.

As the prosecutors discussed the growing heroin traffic in the city — Mr. Johnson said there were between 400,000 and 800,000 addicts here — Mr. Leval observed that though the narcotics sales were increasing steadily, the money allocated to fight these crimes was being cut sharply.

Sources close to Mr. Johnson said it was impossible even to make a good guess about the amount of money taken in by heroin sales in New York City, but that it certainly was in the billions of dollars annually.

The investigation of what Mr. Santucci called "the Far East connection," had to contend with a code that used such words as "food," and "books," for narcotics. And to explain arrangements for customers, one defendant told another: "Just tell them the people said you know that the landlord is getting it together; he's painting and everything."

ALLEGED THREAT IS DESCRIBED

The reference to the planned murder of Mr. Barnes in the indictment said:

"On or about the fall, 1975, in the Manhattan Correctional Center, 150 Park Row, New York County, co-conspirator Warren Sims and defendant Frank Lucas discussed killing Leroy Barnes, also known as 'Nicky,' in order to eliminate heroin competition to the Lucas brothers' organization."

Three brothers of the alleged head of the heroin ring were indicted. They were Lawrence, Vernon and Ezell Lucas. Among the others indicted were a minister, a lawyer, a nurse and a school matron.

Convict Ran Drug Ring

BY THE NEW YORK TIMES | SEPT. 17, 1977

FRANK LUCAS, ONE of New York City's major drug dealers, has admitted running a multimillion-dollar drug ring while in prison on other charges.

Sterling Johnson Jr., the city's special narcotics prosecutor, said Mr. Lucas had admitted that he ran the drug ring from his cell in the Metropolitan Correctional Center with the help of his brothers, Lawrence, 39 years old, of Queens and Ezell, 26, of Wilson, N.C.

Mr. Lucas, 43, his brothers and 26 others were indicted last April as alleged … participants in a loosely knit operation that smuggled narcotics into the United States from Thailand.

"I was the boss," Mr. Lucas told Justice Michael J. Dontzen of State Supreme Court in Manhattan on Sept. 7, Mr. Johnson said. From his cell he allegedly oversaw the purchasing, processing and financing of the ring's activities.

The younger Lucas brothers have also reportedly admitted their participation in the ring.

A New Jersey Crime Story's Hollywood Ending

BY RICHARD G. JONES | NOV. 1, 2007

WEST CALDWELL, N.J., OCT. 31 — It was the early 1970s, and every week nearly four dozen American soldiers were returning home from Vietnam in flag-draped coffins. Frank Lucas, who ruled a crime empire in Newark and Harlem, had a plan: smuggle the purest Asian heroin he could find into New York, stashed inside those coffins.

It took Richard M. Roberts, a prosecutor in Essex County, until 1975 to catch on to the scheme, and a year after that he helped put together the case that would earn Mr. Lucas a sentence of 70 years to life in federal prison. Mr. Lucas returned the favor by putting out a $100,000 contract on Mr. Roberts's life.

The contract was never carried out, and Mr. Lucas, who turned government informant, was freed after serving seven years. He said that as he spent day after day in prison, the notion of becoming an informant, and shortening his sentence, became more appealing. Information he provided would help lead to scores of convictions, including cases against corrupt police officers, and an unlikely friendship between Mr. Lucas and Mr. Roberts developed.

Now, Mr. Roberts — who is known as Richie — and Mr. Lucas talk almost every day, and they usually meet once a week at Mr. Roberts's expansive law office here. Mr. Roberts also is the godfather to Mr. Lucas's son, Ray, 11, and helps to pay for the child's education.

They are friends who finish each other's sentences, and they share recollections about the days when Mr. Lucas's Newark gang — whose members called themselves the Country Boys, because Mr. Lucas was from North Carolina — ruled the drug trade in two states with a deadly form of heroin known as "blue magic."

"I can't explain it," Mr. Roberts said with a shrug and a wan smile

The real Frank Lucas, center, with his wife, Julie, and his son, Ray, in New York City.

when asked about his friendship with Mr. Lucas. "What he did disgusts me. But here we are."

It is the stuff of movies. Indeed, the story of Mr. Roberts's successful pursuit and prosecution of Mr. Lucas is the subject of the film "American Gangster," which is being released on Friday, with Russell Crowe as Mr. Roberts and Denzel Washington as Mr. Lucas. As their friendship has been thrust into the spotlight, each has responded in a way that seems out of character.

Mr. Lucas, 77, who favored chinchilla coats when he ran his drug empire, has recoiled from the publicity that has come with the movie.

"I'm not working today, no comment," he said when a reporter called for an interview last week, before handing the telephone to his daughter, Francine.

And Mr. Roberts, the prosecutor and former undercover investigator who favored the shadows, has embraced his star turn, if somewhat reluctantly.

"There are so many conflicting aspects of this," said Mr. Roberts, a silver-haired, compact man whose lawyerly diction is still influenced by his Bronx upbringing. "People are focusing on some of the wrong things when it comes to Frank."

Mr. Lucas's story is like that of any gangster's rise through the ranks, except that it is seen through the lens of racial prejudice in the criminal world.

Mr. Lucas, who is black, was believed to be one of the first Americans to establish a direct relationship with drug suppliers overseas. After making a connection in Southeast Asia, he brokered a deal in which more than $50 million of high-quality heroin — which officials said was up to 10 times more potent than what had been available on the street in the 1970s — was smuggled into the United States, much of it stashed in secret compartments that were built into the coffins of dead soldiers.

"If you had a connection, you were the king, and Frank was the king," said Judge Sterling Johnson Jr. of the Federal District Court in Brooklyn. In the mid-1970s, he was a special prosecutor dealing in narcotics cases in New York City and, with Mr. Roberts, was part of a two-state effort to topple Mr. Lucas.

"In those days we were inundated with drugs," Judge Johnson said. "We would make arrests, but it was like digging a hole in the ocean. No matter what you did, there's always someone there to replace them."

Mr. Roberts joined the Essex County prosecutor's office as a detective in 1963. In 1971, after earning a law degree from Seton Hall University, he became a prosecutor, and two years later, he was asked to lead the office's special narcotics squad. In 1975 — in large part because of the work of Mr. Roberts and Mr. Johnson — Mr. Lucas was arrested; he was convicted on federal drug charges a year later.

"American Gangster" depicts Mr. Roberts' pursuit of Mr. Lucas. Mr. Roberts, now a lawyer in private practice, said that he was satisfied that the film and its director, Ridley Scott, have not glorified Mr. Lucas's life and times. But he was concerned that young people in

Mr. Roberts, in his West Caldwell, N.J., office, is now a friend of Mr. Lucas, the drug supplier he helped bring down.

the rough neighborhoods of Newark might celebrate the swagger and short-lived success of Mr. Lucas.

"A lot of people are drawn to the idea that a black man was able to rise to that height over a white man — the Mafia — because of his brains," Mr. Roberts said. "That's fine. I'm Jewish, and part of me thinks that Bugsy Siegel and Meyer Lansky were pretty cool guys because at a time when everybody thought that Jews were wimps, these guys rose to the heights of the Mafia. Part of me does feel that.

"But the other part of me recognizes that this is ridiculous; these guys are killers, not to be admired," he added. "It's the same thing with Frank. In truth, Frank Lucas has probably destroyed more black lives than the K.K.K. could ever dream of."

Steven Zaillian, who wrote the screenplay for "American Gangster," said that thought helped shape how he depicted the Lucas character in the film.

"When you meet Frank, he's very charismatic, very personable," said Mr. Zaillian, who interviewed both men extensively. "But you can never forget who he is and what he's done."

It was while the case against Mr. Lucas was being prepared that Mr. Roberts learned that Mr. Lucas had put out a contract on his life.

He briefly carried a pistol just in case — including into courtrooms, the gun tucked in an ankle holster: "I thought I was going to shoot my toes off."

As the opening of "American Gangster" approached, Mr. Roberts was the subject of several celebrations — including one held by the alumni association at Weequahic High School in Newark, which sponsored a screening of the film last week as a cautionary tale for students — and he attended the film's premiere in Harlem last month. Mr. Lucas skipped the premiere and has declined most interview requests.

Mr. Zaillian said he reached out to Mr. Lucas after the premiere. "He said, 'I know what I am, I know what I did.' "

Frank Lucas Dies at 88; Drug Kingpin Depicted in 'American Gangster'

BY ROBERT D. MCFADDEN | MAY 31, 2019

AS THE VIETNAM WAR raged in the late 1960s and early '70s, a potent heroin called "Blue Magic" flooded into Harlem and Newark from a mysterious Southeast Asian connection. It destroyed lives, and it turned a black gangster named Frank Lucas into one of America's most notorious drug kingpins.

His life of crime — rising from poverty to riches in an enterprise that succeeded beyond his wildest dreams — was portrayed in 2007 in Ridley Scott's film "American Gangster," with Denzel Washington as Mr. Lucas and Russell Crowe as the prosecutor who brought him down.

The movie was a Hollywood composite of fact and fiction, depicting Mr. Lucas as a daring, imaginative criminal who set up the Asian connection, smuggled heroin in the coffins of service personnel killed in action, and broke into the Mafia's long domination of narcotics in the New York area — all claims made by Mr. Lucas that have been challenged by investigators and journalists.

Even so, the story of Frank Lucas, who died on Thursday night in Cedar Grove, N.J., at 88, is a larger-than-life tale of ambition, organization and ruthless brutality.

By his own account, he ordered and committed murders, bribed personnel in Vietnam to set up a heroin connection and paid corrupt police officers $200,000 a week. He hobnobbed with Joe Louis, Muhammad Ali, James Brown and Diana Ross, and spent lavishly on cars, clothing, jewelry and entertainment.

At the peak of his empire, he claimed he was taking in $1 million a day, had $52 million stashed in Cayman Islands banks and $300 million in stockpiled heroin, and owned office buildings in Detroit, a cattle ranch in North Carolina and apartments in New York, Miami, Los Angeles and Puerto Rico.

It all collapsed in 1975. Arrested at his New Jersey home, where $584,000 in cash was found, he was convicted of federal drug charges in New York and state charges in New Jersey and sentenced to 70 years in prison.

He served only seven years, however, after providing information that led to the convictions of scores of associates and crooked officials.

His death was confirmed by his nephew Aldwan Lassiter in a telephone interview.

Mr. Lucas's survivors include four daughters, Francine Lucas-Sinclair and Ruby, Betty and Candace Lucas; two sons, Frank Jr. and Tony Walters; many grandchildren and great-grandchildren; two sisters, Mattie Lassiter and Emma Moye; and three brothers, Ezell, Lawrence and LeVon Lucas. His wife, Julie, and another son, Ray, died before him.

Richard M. Roberts, who led the prosecution of Mr. Lucas in New Jersey, had befriended him in recent years but was under no illusions about what he did long ago. "In truth," Mr. Roberts told The New York Times in 2007, "Frank Lucas has probably destroyed more black lives than the K.K.K. could ever dream of."

Frank Lucas was born in La Grange, N.C., on Sept. 9, 1930, to Fred and Mahalee (Jones) Lucas. He had almost no formal education, and as a boy he mugged drunks. At 15 he assaulted a man, stole $400 and fled to New York. He was soon gambling and selling drugs in Harlem; his crimes later escalated to armed robberies.

He established street credibility in 1966 by shooting a notoriously tough drug dealer on a crowded sidewalk four times in the head. "Bam! Bam! Bam! Bam!" he told Mark Jacobson for a 2000 New York magazine profile that was a basis for "American Gangster." He was never prosecuted for that crime, which he later denied committing.

But he had caught the eye of Ellsworth Johnson, who controlled gambling and extortion rackets in Harlem. Mr. Lucas claimed that Mr. Johnson, who was known as Bumpy, became his mentor. Others disputed this. But after Mr. Johnson died in 1968, Mr. Lucas developed his lucrative criminal enterprise.

In accounts to the authorities, he said that to break the Mafia monopoly on heroin supplies, which were sold in Harlem and Newark by black dealers, he flew to Thailand and met Leslie Atkinson, known as Ike, a North Carolinian married to one of Mr. Lucas's cousins. He said that Mr. Atkinson, who ran a Bangkok bar and sold drugs to black soldiers, agreed to help.

In the Golden Triangle, at the borders of Thailand, Burma and Laos, Mr. Lucas said, they made a deal with a Chinese-Thai man named Luchai Rubiwat, who grew poppies and processed opium into almost pure heroin. Mr. Lucas said he bought 132 kilos, or 290 pounds, for $4,300 a kilo. In Harlem, he said, the Mafia would have charged $50,000 a kilo, which would sell for $300,000 on the street.

Disguised as an Army officer, Mr. Lucas said, he organized a network of bribed soldiers to move heroin to an air base in Vietnam, from which the bodies of servicemen were flown home. He said he hired a carpenter to build coffins with false bottoms to conceal heroin.

Mr. Atkinson later disputed Mr. Lucas's account; the heroin, he said, was smuggled in teak furniture in an operation he controlled. Ron Chepesiuk, the author of the book "Superfly: The True Untold Story of Frank Lucas, the American Gangster" (2007), contended in a 2008 article in the online journal New Criminologist that Mr. Atkinson, not Mr. Lucas, had made the connection. He also quoted investigators as saying that many of Mr. Lucas's claims were bogus.

But the movie reflected Mr. Lucas's account of coffins arriving at military bases in the United States, where confederates retrieved the heroin and moved it to Harlem. There, Mr. Lucas said, the drug was cut from 98 percent purity to 10 or 12 percent, double the strength of other brands on the streets.

His "Blue Magic" sold primarily on West 116th Street, between Seventh and Eighth Avenues, and the area became an open supermarket for drugs.

Investigated by task forces of federal, state and city authorities in New York and New Jersey, Mr. Lucas was arrested in a raid at his home in Teaneck, N.J., on Jan. 28, 1975. Despite the murders of two witnesses who had testified against him before a grand jury, Mr. Lucas was convicted in federal court in New York and in Essex County, N.J.

His cooperation in a wider inquiry led to his release in 1982. He was convicted of new drug charges in 1984 and imprisoned until 1991.

His illicit assets were confiscated by the government in the 1970s, and he lived anonymously in the federal witness protection program for years. He was a paid consultant for "American Gangster." With Aliya S. King, he wrote an autobiography, "Original Gangster," published by St. Martin's Press in 2010.

Living in Newark and using a wheelchair in recent years, he professed remorse for his crimes and helped his daughter in an organization that aided children of imprisoned parents. He promised to use the proceeds from his book to promote education, and dedicated the book to his family and to "all the kids who will read it."

"Please learn from my mistakes," he admonished young readers. "Stay in school, finish high school and earn the highest degree in education that you can. This is the way to go in life."

DANIEL E. SLOTNIK contributed reporting.

CHAPTER 5

The Global Empire of Paul Le Roux

For years, D.E.A. prosecutors in the Midwest suspected there was a vast, unknown global drug empire that operated entirely in anonymity. Their investigation led them to a mild-mannered programmer and early dot-com pioneer turned pharmaceutical executive. His company, RX Limited, operated as a legal incorporated entity in the United States, selling discounted prescriptions. As federal law enforcement and NATO investigators eventually discovered, this was not the executive's only business venture. Between 2000 and 2017, the former head of RX Limited was the world's largest drug trafficker. He employed entire armies, ordered military coups and changed the geopolitical landscape throughout much of Africa and East Asia. It was only after the assassination of a close colleague that we would learn his name: Paul Le Roux.

Ex-Soldier Became Contract Killer, Authorities Say

BY BENJAMIN WEISER | SEPT. 27, 2013

HIS NICKNAME WAS RAMBO. He was a sergeant in the Army, and he trained soldiers to be snipers. But after leaving the military in 2004, the authorities say, he put his skills to work in a less honorable way: earning a living as a contract killer.

This past spring, the onetime sergeant, Joseph Hunter, 48, and two other former soldiers agreed to murder an agent of the United States

Drug Enforcement Administration and one of that agency's confidential informers, both in Liberia, for a total of $800,000, federal prosecutors said on Friday in Manhattan.

The plot had been proposed by men who held themselves out as Colombian drug traffickers, an indictment says.

"My guys will handle it," Mr. Hunter wrote in an e-mail on May 30, responding to a question as to whether his team would be willing to carry out the killings, the indictment charges.

In fact, the authorities said, the purported drug traffickers were confidential sources for the D.E.A. and part of an undercover sting operation that ultimately led to the arrests of Mr. Hunter and two others: another former American Army sergeant, Timothy Vamvakias, 42, and a former German corporal, Dennis Gogel, 27. All three were charged with conspiracy to murder the agent and the informer, as well as conspiring to import cocaine into the United States.

Two other men, Michael Filter, 29, and Slawomir Soborski, 40, who served in the German and Polish militaries, respectively, have also been arrested and charged in the drug trafficking conspiracy, prosecutors said. They are awaiting extradition from Estonia, the authorities said.

"The charges tell a tale of an international band of mercenary marksmen who enlisted their elite military training to serve as hired guns for evil ends," Preet Bharara, the United States attorney for the Southern District of New York, said at a news conference on Friday.

Mr. Bharara described the charges with Derek Maltz, who heads the D.E.A.'s special operations division.

Mr. Hunter referred to contract assassinations euphemistically as "bonus work" or "bonus jobs," the indictment says, adding that he told the confidential informers that he had done such work before. Mr. Bharara said Mr. Hunter had successfully arranged for the murders "of numerous people," though he did not name them.

The indictment says that Mr. Hunter began collecting résumés for prospective members of his so-called security team, which had

Joseph Hunter in custody in Thailand. He and two others were accused of agreeing to kill a federal drug agent and an informer.

planned to use pistols and submachine guns, with silencers, to carry out the murders. Mr. Gogel told one of the drug agency informers that the murders could be made to resemble an ordinary street crime, "like a bad robbery or anything, you know," the indictment says.

Mr. Hunter told co-conspirators that they would be working for a Colombian cartel and that they could expect to "see tons of cocaine and millions of dollars," the indictment says. They would also have the opportunity to participate in assassinations, he told them, according to the indictment. "Most of the bonus work is up close … because in the cities … you don't get long-range shots," the indictment quotes him as saying.

Part of an escape plan involved the use of sophisticated latex face masks that would make the wearer appear to be of another race, the indictment said.

Mr. Vamvakias, describing the proposed murders of the D.E.A. agent and the informer, was quoted in the indictment as saying, "You know, we gotta do this, hit it hard, hit it fast, make sure it's done," and then leave.

"That's the biggest headache," he added. "The job's not the headache; it's getting in and out."

Mr. Hunter was taken into custody in Thailand, Mr. Bharara said, and was to be arraigned in Manhattan on Saturday. Mr. Vamvakias and Mr. Gogel were each sent to the United States from Liberia and arraigned on Thursday, when they were ordered detained and entered not guilty pleas, the authorities said.

Mr. Vamvakias's lawyer, Bobbi C. Sternheim, said, "We are prepared to vigorously defend" against the charges. Mr. Gogel's lawyer, Edward D. Wilford, declined to comment.

The case, with its use of confidential informers posing as drug traffickers, had echoes of other D.E.A. international sting operations, like the one in 2008 that ensnared the Russian arms trafficker Viktor Bout, who was brought to the United States and tried and convicted in 2011.

Mr. Bharara and Mr. Maltz made it clear that the drug agency had had its eye on Mr. Hunter for some time. After learning about him through a different investigation, Mr. Bharara said, the agency decided "to do something to incapacitate him."

Mr. Maltz said the operation had lasted close to a year. He said the goal was to "be able to take these threats out before something bad happens."

In Real Life, 'Rambo' Ends Up as a Soldier of Misfortune, Behind Bars

BY ALAN FEUER | DEC. 20, 2014

LATE LAST YEAR, a strike force of elite Thai police officers descended on the Baan Suan estates, a palm-treed housing complex next to a golf course on the tourist island of Phuket. The officers' mission was to capture the American expatriate in Villa 34: Joseph Hunter, a retired soldier wanted by his government for having taken up what law enforcement officials called a new career — as a hired killer.

Within three days, Mr. Hunter, a former Army sniper with Special Forces training, was in shackles on an airplane bound for New York, where he was formally accused of managing a team of contract hit men overseas. Law enforcement officials said the group had conspired to murder a federal drug agent and a drug-world informant in exchange for an $800,000 bounty from men they believed were members of a Colombian cartel.

The case against Mr. Hunter, nicknamed Rambo, seemed to have been lifted from the latest action thriller. The hit was set for Liberia and, the Drug Enforcement Administration said, the plans were elaborate; the hired killers asked their employers for sophisticated latex masks to make them look as if they were of a different race and plotted to escape aboard a privately chartered jet. In a more shocking twist, at least for the gunmen, the supposed cartel members employing them were, in reality, D.E.A. agents setting up a sting.

The narrative of the assassination plot may be hard to dispute; Mr. Hunter and his team were caught on audio and video tapes plotting the murders.

But there may be more to the story than the court filings convey. According to Mr. Hunter's family and his lawyer — and to two federal agents, one current and one retired — the person who set the authorities on Mr. Hunter's trail was his former boss, Paul Le Roux, a shadowy South African operator who, until recently, was one of the world's least known but most successful outlaws.

According to the federal agents, Mr. Le Roux was an enterprising criminal who had overseen an empire in illegal guns and drugs that spanned four continents before he turned on Mr. Hunter in an attempt to get a lighter sentence after his own arrest. One of the agents compared Mr. Le Roux, who he said was still in custody, to Viktor Bout, the infamous Russian arms dealer said to be the real-life inspiration for the movie "Lord of War."

"Le Roux is a bad guy, a very bad guy," the agent said, speaking on the condition of anonymity because, he said, Mr. Le Roux's cooperation has been a secret. "He's Viktor Bout on steroids."

Mr. Le Roux's alleged involvement may well complicate what the D.E.A. hoped would be an open-and-shut case against Mr. Hunter, 49, because of the video and audio evidence. Mr. Hunter's lawyer, Marlon Kirton, contends that his client was entrapped and would never have recruited his team of former military men if the government had not launched a sting against him, after the tip from Mr. Le Roux. Prosecutors contend, however, that Mr. Hunter was caught on tape boasting of having killed two people in the Philippines before the latest plot was hatched, which could complicate an entrapment defense.

Attempts to find a lawyer representing Mr. Le Roux were unsuccessful. There are no public federal documents related to his arrest or alleged cooperation, nor are there references to him in Mr. Hunter's public court file, which notes that many files are sealed.

Even before Mr. Le Roux reportedly became a government informant, Mr. Hunter's story was an elaborate tale of international intrigue — of soldiers and soldiers of fortune — that began somewhat improbably in Owensboro, Ky., a tobacco manufacturing hub two hours outside Louisville. Mr. Hunter grew up there and returned in mid-2004 after retiring from the Army.

Not unlike many veterans, Mr. Hunter made a difficult discovery when he got home: It was hard to find civilian work he liked and that made use of the skills he had developed over two decades in uniform.

"He was miserable, frustrated beyond belief," said his sister, Karen Adams, who lives in Owensboro. Her brother, she recounted, tried to find work as a police officer and as a United States marshal, but she said he was rejected because he was considered too old at 38 even though he was in great shape from weight lifting and martial-arts training.

In 2005, she said, Mr. Hunter reluctantly accepted a position as an inmate counselor at the Green River Correctional Complex, a county prison more than an hour's drive from Owensboro. He hated it, she said — the drudgery, the physical confinement — and lasted only 15 months.

Looking for a paycheck, and the adrenaline rush of a war zone, he went back, she said, to the type of work he knew best, signing up with DynCorp International, a private security firm. According to Ms. Adams, DynCorp sent him to Iraq, where he worked taking finger-prints and DNA swabs from company employees. Two years later, he joined another firm in Iraq called Triple Canopy, protecting American embassy workers, she said.

It was in 2009, as he became enmeshed in the chummy, macho world of contract security work, that another soldier for hire intro-duced him to a charismatic businessman named Paul Le Roux, accord-ing to Mr. Hunter's sister. She said that Mr. Le Roux promptly offered her brother a job.

Thus began a three-year stint of travel during which she said Mr. Hunter accompanied Mr. Le Roux on business trips to Brazil, the Republic of Congo, Mali and the Philippines. He was making good money, his sister said, and those who knew him seemed impressed, though perhaps a bit confused, by his glamorous new job.

"All he told me was that he was guarding some millionaire on a yacht, cruising around in Africa," said Bill Boyd, a fellow Army vet-eran from Owensboro and one of Mr. Hunter's oldest friends. "The guy supposedly traded in commodities, and Joe was acting as his bodyguard."

But according to the federal agents, Mr. Le Roux traded in far more than commodities. The agents confirmed that Mr. Le Roux had been the architect of a prescription pill scheme, with roots in Minnesota and Brazil, in which physicians employed by him provided painkillers to be sold on the Internet. Mr. Le Roux was never named or charged in the case, but both agents acknowledged that he was an unindicted co-conspirator and that he had provided information that led to the indictment of 11 people.

Other authorities also had their eyes on Mr. Le Roux, who is believed to be in his 40s. In July 2011, the United Nations accused him of spending $3 million, including almost $1 million in militia salaries, in violation of an arms embargo in Somalia, adding that one of his partners was also involved in a plot to cultivate hallucinogenic plants at a secret compound near the Ethiopian border.

"Le Roux's businesses were huge," said Lachlan McConnell, a security contractor, now based in the Philippines, who is facing charges of helping Mr. Le Roux with the painkiller scheme. "He had operations in Manila, Hong Kong, Colombia, Africa, Brazil. It was guns, gold, drugs, you name it. It was big, really big."

It remains unclear how much Mr. Hunter knew about his boss's portfolio, but according to his own account furnished to a court-approved psychologist, he believed that Paul Le Roux was no legitimate businessman. In the summer of 2009, Mr. Hunter said, Mr. Le Roux dispatched him to guard a merchant vessel, the M/V Captain Ufuk, that was supposedly hauling commercial cargo to the Philippines.

But when Mr. Hunter boarded the ship, "he learned that weapons were to be picked up, and he began suspecting that he was involved in an illegal operation," the psychological evaluation said. The evaluation added that he left the vessel just before it was seized by the Filipino coast guard. A cache of assault rifles was found on board, and officials in Manila filed charges against several people — among them employees of a company in Manila that the United Nations said was run by Mr. Le Roux.

Last week, the captain of the vessel, Lawrence John Burne, was sentenced in absentia — he had jumped bail and fled — for tax evasion related to the gun shipments, according to an online news release from the Philippines Department of Justice. Tax charges in the case are still pending against several of the defendants, including a South African national identified in court documents as John Paul Le Raux.

"Joe was freaked out," his friend, Mr. Boyd, recalled, but feared for his life if he were to quit, his lawyer said. The evaluation said that Mr. Hunter "began to suspect that, since he was the one renting houses and getting business licenses for Mr. Le Roux's companies, he was being set up to potentially 'take the fall' if the illegal arms activities were discovered."

In September 2012, Mr. Le Roux was captured in a secret operation in Liberia, the federal agents said, and was taken into custody by the D.E.A.

Four months later, Mr. Hunter's own troubles started when the D.E.A. sent two undercover agents to meet him in Thailand, posing as members of a Colombian drug cartel.

According to the indictment Mr. Hunter faces, the supposed cartel members offered him a job as their "head of security," a position that required him to put together a team of able men. By early March, the indictment said, Mr. Hunter had used the Internet to assemble a team: Dennis Gogel, 28, and Michael Filter, 30, both of whom had served with the German armed forces; Slawomir Soborski, a 41-year-old Polish veteran; and Timothy Vamvakias, 43, who had served in the United States Army.

All of the men, including Mr. Hunter, have pleaded not guilty.

After giving their recruits surveillance and security work, the undercover agents in May 2013 offered them what they described as "a bonus job" — a paid assignment to kill a D.E.A. agent and a troublesome informant. "They will handle both jobs," Mr. Hunter wrote in an email, the indictment says. "They just need good tools."

And so began a brainstorming session for the hit; Mr. Gogel and Mr. Vamvakias proposed using "machine guns, cyanide or a grenade," according to the indictment. By midsummer, Mr. Hunter had also emailed the agents a wish list of military hardware: two submachine guns with silencers (he asked for "something small"), two .22-caliber pistols ("these are a must") and a .308-caliber rifle with a scope.

By the end of August, it was settled that Mr. Gogel and Mr. Vamvakias would carry out the hit. Two Liberian visas were obtained, and Mr. Hunter emailed his employers, saying that his men would arrive in Africa on Sept. 25.

By the time they landed, he had already been arrested.

This summer, Mr. Hunter, who faces life in prison, appeared for a status conference at Federal District Court in Manhattan. His cheeks looked hollow, and his wrists were shackled to his ankles by a chain.

His lawyer, Mr. Kirton, had recently returned from trips to the Philippines and Africa, where he had gone in search of information about Mr. Le Roux. He says he did not learn much and has relatively little time left to do so.

Mr. Hunter's trial has been scheduled for March 9. One person unlikely to be in attendance: Paul Le Roux.

Murder Plot Suspect Says Boss Threatened His Life

BY ALAN FEUER | JAN. 13, 2015

A FORMER ARMY SNIPER accused of working as a contract killer said in court papers this week that he had been ensnared in the case by his onetime boss, who, he contends, threatened to kill him if he failed to follow orders.

The former sniper, Joseph Hunter, a 20-year veteran with Special Forces training, was arrested in an overseas sting operation by the Drug Enforcement Administration in September 2013 at his rented bungalow in Phuket, Thailand.

After he was extradited to New York, prosecutors unsealed an indictment alleging that Mr. Hunter, who used the nickname Rambo, was the leader of a team of mercenary killers who planned to assassinate an agent for the Drug Enforcement Administration and a government informer for a group of men they believed were Colombian drug traffickers.

Though prosecutors in New York eventually revealed that the traffickers were actually undercover operatives working with the D.E.A., they never disclosed that an international criminal who once employed Mr. Hunter as a bodyguard was the one who set them on Mr. Hunter's trail and who helped start the sting operation. According to federal agents, that employer was a South African drug- and gunrunner named Paul Le Roux, who was one of the world's least known but most successful outlaws before he was arrested by the drug agency and became a cooperating witness.

From the start, the case of Mr. Hunter has been full of cinematic moments and cloak-and-dagger twists. The government contends that he hired four former soldiers — three from Europe and one from the United States — to act as his accomplices and was recorded on tape agreeing to accept an $800,000 bounty to kill the two victims in

Liberia. The assassins, prosecutors say, planned to wear custom rubber masks and then escape the country in a privately chartered jet.

On Monday evening, Mr. Hunter's lawyer, Marlon Kirton, filed a motion to dismiss the case, accusing the prosecution of "outrageous government conduct" for having used Mr. Le Roux as a cooperating witness. While the motion acknowledged that the use of informers "is widespread in the federal courts," Mr. Kirton argued that it "shocks the conscience" that prosecutors used Mr. Le Roux in that capacity when, as the motion claimed, he threatened to kill Mr. Hunter and his family and, moreover, killed two unnamed associates in the past.

In a redacted affidavit that accompanied the motion, Mr. Hunter said Mr. Le Roux had not only threatened his life, but also bragged that he had foreign law-enforcement officers and government officials on his payroll.

Speaking out for the first time since his arrest — if only from jail and by way of the redacted affidavit — Mr. Hunter, 49, wrote that he was in constant fear that Mr. Le Roux would kill him or have him "falsely arrested if I did not do his bidding." The affidavit added: "Everyone was afraid of this man. I was afraid of this man."

A spokeswoman for the United States attorney's office for the Southern District of New York, which is handling Mr. Hunter's case, declined to comment on the documents on Tuesday. The prosecutor's office has repeatedly declined to discuss Mr. Le Roux or his involvement with Mr. Hunter, who is facing life in prison if convicted.

Two of Mr. Hunter's co-defendants have recently pleaded guilty to conspiracy charges related to the case. One of them, Timothy Vamvakias, a former United States Army soldier, entered his guilty plea on Jan. 9. A second, Dennis Gogel, a veteran of the German armed forces, pleaded guilty on Tuesday. Both of their lawyers declined to comment on their pleas. Two other men, Michael Filter, from Germany, and Slawomir Soborski, from Poland, are accused of narcotics charges and conspiracy. Mr. Hunter's trial is scheduled to begin on March 9.

U.S. Reveals Criminal Boss's Role in Capturing a Mercenary

BY ALAN FEUER | FEB. 1, 2015

IN MAY 2013, court papers say, Joseph Hunter, a soldier of fortune, got an email from his boss. The boss, a South African named Paul Le Roux, wanted Mr. Hunter's assistance with "a priority job."

Six months earlier, after sailing out of Ecuador, a 40-foot yacht hired by Mr. Le Roux had crashed on the shores of a South Pacific island. The local police found a dead Slovakian man onboard and $100 million worth of cocaine inside the boat's hull. In the ensuing weeks, Mr. Le Roux wrote to Mr. Hunter, the yacht's captain had turned state's evidence and begun "providing tips" to American authorities.

And so in his email, court papers say, Mr. Le Roux asked Mr. Hunter "to fix this issue." The papers add that Mr. Hunter, in an email of his own, told his boss, "My guys will handle it."

The way that Mr. Hunter, 49, allegedly handled it, by planning to assassinate the captain and an American federal agent, led to his arrest and extradition to New York. But on Friday, for the first time, federal prosecutors acknowledged that the sting operation that led to Mr. Hunter's arrest was launched with the help of Mr. Le Roux himself.

The alleged plans were never carried out, and Mr. Hunter remains imprisoned in New York.

The official disclosure of Mr. Le Roux's involvement in the case, which The New York Times reported in December was contained in documents filed by the government on Friday night in response to arguments by Mr. Hunter's lawyer that the case against his client should be dismissed. In January, the lawyer, Marlon Kirton, filed a motion asserting that the Drug Enforcement Administration had entrapped his client and accusing prosecutors of "outrageous government conduct" for having used Mr. Le Roux as a cooperating witness.

In the filing submitted on Friday, the prosecutors acknowledged that Mr. Le Roux — referred to in the documents as CW-1 — had been arrested by the D.E.A. in September 2012 and had subsequently helped the agency in its pursuit of Mr. Hunter. At the time of his arrest, the documents say, Mr. Le Roux was a veteran outlaw whose crimes included arranging murders, trafficking in methamphetamine, money laundering, mail fraud, wire fraud and "other serious offenses."

Nonetheless, his role in helping to capture Mr. Hunter, who used the nickname Rambo, was not unusual, prosecutors said. "The government's use of a cooperating witness with a violent criminal history is, in fact, commonplace in sting operations targeting narcotics and violent crimes," the prosecutors wrote.

In seeking to rebut Mr. Kirton's accusations of entrapment, the prosecutors argued that Mr. Hunter was not "a fearful victim who was manipulated by the Government to violate the law" but "an active participant" in "murder-for-hire conspiracies." They maintained that Mr. Hunter had killed before, quoting covertly made recordings in which they said he could be heard boasting that, in a single year, he had helped kill nine people on Mr. Le Roux's behalf.

Most of the recordings were made in a house in Phuket, Thailand, where, in March 2013, Mr. Le Roux sent Mr. Hunter, at the D.E.A.'s request, to meet with two undercover operatives who were posing as members of a Colombian drug cartel. Six months later, as a pair of hit men recruited by Mr. Hunter were about to commit the contract killings — in Liberia — the Thai police raided the house in Phuket, arresting Mr. Hunter before his extradition to New York.

Two of Mr. Hunter's co-defendants in the murder-for-hire case, Timothy Vamvakias, a former American soldier, and Dennis Gogel, a German military veteran, pleaded guilty to conspiracy charges last month in Federal District Court in Manhattan. Two other men named in the case, Michael Filter, a retired German soldier, and Slawomir Soborski, who once served in the Polish armed forces, still face narcotics and murder conspiracy charges. They have pleaded not guilty, as has Mr. Hunter. His trial is scheduled to begin on March 9.

Former Army Sniper Pleads Guilty in Murder-for-Hire Conspiracy

BY BENJAMIN WEISER | FEB. 13, 2015

A FORMER ARMY SERGEANT with the nickname Rambo pleaded guilty on Friday to conspiring to murder a federal drug agent and another man, in what the government has said was his post-military role as a contract killer.

The former sergeant, Joseph M. Hunter, 49, who had been a sniper instructor, was arrested in 2013 after he and two other men were ensnared in a sting operation in which they agreed to kill an agent of the United States Drug Enforcement Administration and one of the agency's confidential informers for $800,000.

During the sting operation, Mr. Hunter met with two government informers who were posing as Colombian drug traffickers and who discussed the possibility of Mr. Hunter's serving as the head of security for their organization, a federal indictment charged.

Mr. Hunter later told other men he had recruited that they would be working for a Colombian cartel and "could expect to 'see tons of cocaine and millions of dollars,' " the indictment said.

In May 2013, Mr. Hunter was asked in an email whether his team would be willing to kill the agent and a boat captain who was said to be providing information to the authorities, and he responded, "My guys will handle it," the indictment said.

Mr. Hunter told a judge in Federal District Court in Manhattan on Friday that he had "agreed with others to kill an agent of the U.S. Drug Enforcement Administration" and the informer who was assisting the agent.

In all, Mr. Hunter pleaded guilty to conspiracy charges related to the murder plot, the importation of cocaine into the United States and the possession of a firearm in furtherance of a violent crime.

One of the counts carries a 10-year minimum sentence, and Mr.

Hunter could face life imprisonment when he is sentenced by Judge Laura Taylor Swain on May 29.

"This global gun for hire will now be confined stateside in federal prison," Preet Bharara, the United States attorney for the Southern District of New York, said on Friday.

After the hearing, one of Mr. Hunter's lawyers, Marlon G. Kirton, said of his client's decision to plead guilty, "We think he made the right call."

Mr. Kirton said his client had post-traumatic stress disorder and depression, and hoped to receive "a reasonable sentence so he can go home to his family," in Owensboro, Ky.

"We are grateful that we have an opportunity to ask for 10 years," Mr. Kirton said.

The defense had sought dismissal of the charges on grounds of outrageous government conduct, citing the drug agency's use of a cooperating witness — who was a former boss of Mr. Hunter's and had threatened to kill him — to introduce Mr. Hunter to the informers who were posing as traffickers.

The New York Times reported in December that the former boss was Paul Le Roux, a shadowy South African businessman for whom Mr. Hunter had done security work, accompanying him on trips to Brazil, the Republic of Congo, Mali and the Philippines. In 2012, Mr. Le Roux was taken into custody in Liberia and began cooperating with the United States authorities. The Times was not able to locate a lawyer representing Mr. Le Roux, and the government has not named him in court papers.

Mr. Hunter claimed in a court filing last month that he "was in constant fear" that his former boss "would kill me or have me falsely arrested if I did not do his bidding."

Mr. Bharara's office said Mr. Hunter's contention was meritless, noting that he had not distanced himself from Mr. Le Roux or reported his concerns to law enforcement.

"Hunter was not a fearful victim who was manipulated by the government to violate the law," Mr. Bharara's office wrote. "To the contrary, Hunter was an active and willing participant in the narcotics trafficking and murder-for-hire conspiracies from the beginning."

With Mr. Hunter's plea, the defense claim is now moot.

Two of Mr. Hunter's co-defendants — Timothy Vamvakias, another former Army sergeant, and Dennis Gogel, a former German corporal — have each pleaded guilty in the murder and cocaine importation conspiracies. A third co-defendant, Slawomir Soborski, who once served in the Polish military, has pleaded guilty in the cocaine conspiracy, and a fourth co-defendant still faces trial.

In Spellbinding Testimony, Crime Lord Details Mayhem and Murders

BY ALAN FEUER | APRIL 5, 2018

PAUL LE ROUX, one of the world's least known but most prodigious criminals, emerged from the shadows this week and testified for the first time about the myriad illegal schemes he committed in his 20-year career on the wrong side of the law.

In a spellbinding two-day turn as a prosecution witness, Mr. Le Roux confessed to an astonishing array of crimes. He said he had once sold missile technology to Iran, shipped guns from Indonesia, and trafficked methamphetamines out of North Korea. He calmly told a jury in New York that he had taken part in at least five murders. With a businesslike demeanor, he admitted not only to arming a 200-man militia in Somalia but also to hatching plans to use mercenaries to overthrow the government of the Seychelles.

When a prosecutor asked what he had smuggled over the years, Mr. Le Roux responded without affect: "Cash, chemicals, drugs and gold." He said that he had also smuggled weapons and when asked to whom, he answered: "Rebels, warlords, criminals — essentially anyone who had money."

A South African businessman with illicit interests that spanned four continents, Mr. Le Roux recounted all of this at the murder conspiracy trial of three soldiers-of-fortune on his payroll who stand accused of killing a Filipino real-estate agent in 2012. The agent, Catherine Lee, was shot in the face while taking two of the defendants, Adam Samia and Carl D. Stillwell, on a tour of properties near Manila, prosecutors say, after which her body was dumped on a pile of garbage. Joseph Hunter, the third defendant at the trial in Federal District Court in Manhattan, was charged with overseeing the assassination.

Silver-haired and hulking in his prison-issue shirt, Mr. Le Roux spoke about Ms. Lee in his first few moments on the stand, saying he had ordered her murder because he believed she had stolen from him. "I had her killed," he said matter-of-factly, adding that Mr. Hunter handled the details and that Mr. Samia and "a partner" did the actual work.

The chilling testimony was part of Mr. Le Roux's cooperation with the government. In late 2012, he was arrested by the Drug Enforcement Administration after being lured to Liberia. Ever since, Mr. Le Roux, 45, has been assisting the authorities in rounding up the members of his sprawling organization in an effort to reduce a possible life sentence.

In 2013, he helped the D.E.A. launch a sting operation in Thailand that led to Mr. Hunter's first arrest and eventual sentence of 20 years in prison. In that case, the drug agency caught Mr. Hunter and three others agreeing to murder one of its agents and an informant. Because the charges included a plot to bring cocaine to New York, the case was handled by prosecutors in Manhattan. They are also handling Ms. Lee's murder, claiming it evolved from the same investigation.

The trial so far has focused on the car bombs, arsons and assassinations that Mr. Le Roux employed to protect his smuggling routes — violence that was previewed so unnervingly in opening arguments on Tuesday that a juror told the judge she feared for her safety and was excused the following day.

The trial has also pulled back the veil on the covert world of mercenary work. Mr. Le Roux testified that he paid his guns-for-hire $5,000 to $10,000 a month, plus expenses. He said he paid an extra $25,000 for "bonus work," which he described as "acts of killing and any other acts of violence."

"The word 'mercenary,' " he explained, "means a trained person with military experience and an aggressive posture who will beat, shoot, intimidate or kill anyone on instruction."

On Wednesday afternoon, Mr. Le Roux said that for two years his chief mercenary was a man named David Smith who in 2008 formed a company called Echelon Associates to recruit what amounted to a private Praetorian guard. Its members traveled the globe — from Mozambique to Papua New Guinea — often using false passports and code names like Daddy Mac and Rambo to scout locations for Mr. Le Roux, watch his assets and maim or murder on his behalf.

Among those murdered was Mr. Smith, Mr. Le Roux admitted. He said he had his henchman killed in 2010 after finding out that Mr. Smith was cheating him. Mr. Le Roux subsequently named Mr. Hunter his security chief.

A former Army sergeant with Special Forces training, Mr. Hunter, 52, had served in the military and with two private security firms in Iraq. During the sting in Thailand, he was caught on camera boasting of the vicious acts he committed for Mr. Le Roux: how he waterboarded one man, shot a second in the hand and pitched a third — another suspected thief — overboard at sea.

On Thursday, Mr. Le Roux testified that after two men on his hit team — a gunman from New Zealand and a former member of the French Foreign Legion — quit their jobs, he instructed Mr. Hunter to replace them. Mr. Hunter, emails show, reached out to Mr. Samia, a onetime Army sniper, who lived near Mr. Stillwell, a firearms instructor, in the small town of Roxboro, N.C.

Flight records indicate that Mr. Samia, 43, and Mr. Stillwell, 50, flew to Manila in January 2011, where, Mr. Le Roux recalled, he supplied the men with a rifle (for long shots), a pistol (for close-range shots) and an MP5 submachine gun from a weapons warehouse he maintained. He also gave them Ms. Lee's address.

One month later, Mr. Le Roux said, the two men followed the plan he had concocted: posing as real-estate buyers, they lured Ms. Lee in a Toyota van into the countryside near Las Piñas. Mr. Stillwell later told the D.E.A. that he was driving the van as Mr. Samia fired the pistol into Ms. Lee's face.

In early March, Mr. Hunter drove both men to the airport and put them on a plane, Mr. Le Roux said. Three years later, the D.E.A. tracked them down in Roxboro — with arrest warrants.

Guns, Drugs and Money: Taking Down the Drug Kingpin Paul Le Roux

REVIEW | BY ALAN FEUER | MARCH 15, 2019

THE MASTERMIND
Drugs. Empire. Murder. Betrayal.
By Evan Ratliff
Illustrated. 480 pp. Random House. $28.

WORLD-CLASS CRIMINALS, like world-class writers, are natural obsessives. Alone in their rooms, they both spin endless plots, picking at the details of their projects.

Near the start of "The Mastermind," Evan Ratliff's possessed true-crime investigation, there is a stop-and-gawk image of the obsessive outlaw with whom he becomes obsessed: Paul Le Roux, the South African kingpin who gives the work its title. The scene takes place in a thriller-worthy setting — a penthouse condo in Manila, where Le Roux has based his illegal organization. But when one of Ratliff's sources enters the apartment, he finds the potbellied crime lord in the most unlikely guise: dressed in shorts and flip-flops and perched behind a desk in a room filled with digital servers.

The 300 fever-heated pages that ensue are, in a sense, the author's agitated — and sometimes self-imperiling — attempt to understand that bizarre tableau and to figure out how Paul Le Roux transformed himself, in the course of 30 years, from a teenage tech geek with a talent for encryption to an international villain with a cadre of mercenaries protecting his interests in everything from Congolese gold to North Korean meth. Ratliff's journey is not just one of miles logged on the ground, but of incomparable oddness. In his hunt for those who knew Le Roux, he goes to Minnesota, the Philippines, Israel, Brazil and Vietnam, encountering a cast of characters out of a Coen brothers film: a grizzled Canadian security operative, an elderly pharmacist, a target-shooting Filipino cop, a South African hit man and the pseud-onymous informant who ran Le Roux's business in Somalia and later helped the American authorities to capture him.

The narrator fixed on an elusive prey has been a well-worn device at least since "Moby-Dick," but if there were ever a subject worthy of investigative mania, it is Paul Le Roux. The man was into anything and everything: high-speed yachts, precious metals, plastic explosives, tuna fishing, piracy, Predator drones, Peruvian cocaine and hallucinogens. "He wanted to be the king of his country," according to the informant who ultimately brought him down. "The big man. Sitting on his fat ass behind a giant desk in his palace."

In the midst of his pursuit, Ratliff — like a serial-killer fan boy — tapes multicolored Post-it notes to his bedroom wall in an effort to understand his protagonist's sprawling empire. "I'd like to claim that this was some kind of linear process, a journalist-turned-detective expertly following a trail of bread crumbs down the path to a secret lair," he writes. "But, in truth, people and stories came to me scatter-shot, and I found myself constantly circling back to re-evaluate some fact that I'd been told before."

One of the pleasures of "The Mastermind" is the way in which the story effortlessly toggles between the mundane and the macabre. Le Roux's chief business — and the source of his great wealth — was, for several years, an online pharmacy network. Unsuspecting customers would place their orders for painkillers like Tramadol to call centers run by a company known as RX Limited. Licensed doctors, most in the United States, would evaluate the requests and — unaware of where the payments were going — authorize prescriptions to be handed out by pharmacists from Brooklyn to Wisconsin.

While some of the money was siphoned off along the way to keep the pill mill (and its largely unwitting participants) in motion, the bulk of it was hoarded by Le Roux to fund the rest of his illicit operations. This trick of funneling quasi-legal profits into wholly illegal business ventures eventually led to the crime lord's downfall as investigators dug into the innards of his scheme. It also provided Ratliff with the philosophical ballast of his story. Violent crime, he notes, often exists in vertiginous proximity to ordinary life.

"Call center managers in Tel Aviv could wake up and find themselves arms dealers," he writes. "Family doctors could turn into conspirators in an international drug cartel at the click of a button."

This "adjacent reality," as Ratliff calls it, is Le Roux's reality, and in "The Mastermind" it "lurks just outside of our everyday perception, in the dark corners of the internet we never visit, the quiet ports where ships slip by in the night, the back room of the clinic down the street." There is an inference and perhaps even a lesson here: Bad things happen when the edges of those two worlds start to touch.

Ratliff's book emerged from several articles he wrote for the online magazine The Atavist. Three weeks after "The Mastermind" was published, a second book, Elaine Shannon's **HUNTING LEROUX (Morrow, $27.99),** came out. Shannon, a journalist, has worked closely in the past with the Drug Enforcement Administration and she clearly had access to the two elite agents who helped take down Le Roux. But her book is less broadly sourced than Ratliff's — and not as haunting.

A quick disclaimer: I, too, became obsessed with Le Roux after chasing him and his spectral story for The New York Times years ago. (In "The Mastermind," the author briefly mentions the articles I wrote.) Much like Ratliff, I recall the bleary nights on Google thinking I'd struck gold when I stumbled across Le Roux's name in incorporation papers for a mysterious firm in Hong Kong or a United Nations dossier on the Somalian arms trade. I also recall the nausea that gripped me when Le Roux slipped back into the shadows, and the gold I thought I'd found turned into mist.

All of which is to say that, aside from the other triumphs of "The Mastermind," Ratliff clearly deserves this year's Award for Dogged Journalism for staying on his target until the very end. Without spoiling his story, the end arrives with yet another twist when, after years of living out of sight, Le Roux shows up, in the flesh, in two separate federal courtrooms.

Ratliff's efforts fail only when he tries to lash his story to sweeping themes (Le Roux as the first great outlaw of the digital age) or to root it in current events (Le Roux's supposed role in heightening the opioid crisis). While both of these ideas are likely true, they struck me as the sort of unnecessary stretches that a publishing executive might suggest.

The fact is, Ratliff's tale is unique, so strange and so compelling, it is almost better left to float alone in its cloud of "adjacent reality." That, of course, is where it already exists — close to, but just beyond, the world we recognize: out there, on its own, in a state of shimmering drift.

ALAN FEUER covers crime and criminals for The Times.

Glossary

bribe Money or favor given or promised in order to influence the judgment or conduct of a person in a position of trust.

Bureau of Alcohol, Tobacco and Firearms Otherwise known as the A.T.F., this law enforcement agency of the U.S. Department of Justice includes the investigation and prevention of the illegal use and trafficking of firearms, the illegal use and storage of explosives, acts of arson and bombings, acts of terrorism and the illegal diversion of alcohol and tobacco products.

cartel A combination of independent commercial or industrial enterprises designed to limit competition or fix prices.

dealer A person who buys and sells drugs illegally.

Department of Justice The department of the U.S. government responsible for the enforcement of the law and administration of justice in the United States, equivalent to the justice or interior ministries of other countries.

drug lord The head of an organization or network involved in illegal drug trafficking.

extradition The procedure by which a state or nation, upon receipt of a formal request by another state or nation, turns over to that second jurisdiction an individual charged with or convicted of a crime in that jurisdiction.

F.A.R.C. The Fuerza Alternativa Revolucionaria del Común (the Revolutionary Armed Forces of Colombia — People's Army) was Colombia's largest rebel military group, operating from 1964 to 2017.

Homeland Security Investigations An investigative branch of the Department of Homeland Security.

indictment In law, a formal accusation initiating a criminal case, presented by a grand jury and usually required for felonies and other serious crimes.

informant An individual who secretly provides information to police, the F.B.I. or another law enforcement agency.

kingpin The chief person in a group or undertaking.

laundering The transferring of illegally obtained money or investments through an outside party to conceal the true source.

Medellín cartel A Colombian drug cartel, founded in the city of Medellín, Colombia, under the auspices of Pablo Escobar. The drug cartel operated throughout the 1970s and 1980s in Bolivia, Colombia, Panama, Peru and the United States, as well as in Canada and Europe.

narcotic A drug or other substance, usually addictive, that alters one's mood or behavior and is sold for nonmedical purposes.

Sinaloa cartel Arguably the most powerful drug trafficking organization in the world, this cartel, based in Mexico, is reportedly the largest exporter of heroin and cocaine in the world. Joaquín Guzmán Loera ("El Chapo") led the cartel from 1995 until his extradition to the United States in 2017.

smuggle To import or export secretly contrary to the law and especially without paying duties imposed by law.

trafficking To trade or deal in a specific commodity or service, often of an illegal nature.

Media Literacy Terms

"Media literacy" refers to the ability to access, understand, critically assess and create media. The following terms are important components of media literacy, and they will help you critically engage with the articles in this title.

angle The aspect of a news story that a journalist focuses on and develops.

attribution The method by which a source is identified or by which facts and information are assigned to the person who provided them.

balance Principle of journalism that both perspectives of an argument should be presented in a fair way.

bias A disposition of prejudice in favor of a certain idea, person or perspective.

byline Name of the writer, usually placed between the headline and the story.

commentary A type of story that is an expression of opinion on recent events by a journalist generally known as a commentator.

credibility The quality of being trustworthy and believable, said of a journalistic source.

critical review A type of story that describes an event or work of art, such as a theater performance, film, concert, book, restaurant, radio or television program, exhibition or musical piece, and offers critical assessment of its quality and reception.

editorial Article of opinion or interpretation.

human interest story A type of story that focuses on individuals and how events or issues affect their life, generally offering a sense of relatability to the reader.

impartiality Principle of journalism that a story should not reflect a journalist's bias and should contain balance.

intention The motive or reason behind something, such as the publication of a news story.

interview story A type of story in which the facts are gathered primarily by interviewing another person or persons.

news story An article or style of expository writing that reports news, generally in a straightforward fashion and without editorial comment.

op-ed An opinion piece that reflects a prominent individual's opinion on a topic of interest.

paraphrase The summary of an individual's words, with attribution, rather than a direct quotation of their exact words.

plagiarism An attempt to pass another person's work as one's own without attribution.

quotation The use of an individual's exact words indicated by the use of quotation marks and proper attribution.

reliability The quality of being dependable and accurate, said of a journalistic source.

rhetorical device Technique in writing intending to persuade the reader or communicate a message from a certain perspective.

source The origin of the information reported in journalism.

style A distinctive use of language in writing or speech; also a news or publishing organization's rules for consistent use of language with regard to spelling, punctuation, typography and capitalization, usually regimented by a house style guide.

tone A manner of expression in writing or speech.

Media Literacy Questions

1. Analyze Azam Ahmed's reporting in "El Chapo, Escaped Mexican Drug Lord, Is Recaptured in Gun Battle" (on page 14) and "El Chapo, Mexican Drug Kingpin, Is Extradited to U.S." (on page 23). Do you think he is more impartial in his reporting in one article than the other? If so, why do you think so?

2. The article "El Chapo Puts the Drug War on Trial" (on page 42) is an example of an op-ed. Identify how Ioan Grillo's attitude and tone help convey his opinion on the topic.

3. In "Colombia Marvels at Drug Kingpin: A Chain-Saw Killer, Too?" (on page 77), James Brooke directly quotes some sources while paraphrasing others. What are the strengths of the use of a direct quote as opposed to a paraphrase? What are the weaknesses?

4. Identify the various sources cited in the article "The Long War of Genaro García Luna" (on page 104). How does Daniel Kurtz-Phelan attribute information to each of these sources in his article? How effective are Kurtz-Phelan's attributions in helping the reader identify his sources?

5. Identify each of the sources in "Colombia Starts to Feel Side Effects of Drug Trade" (on page 133) as a primary source or a secondary source. Evaluate the reliability and credibility of each source. How does your evaluation of each source change your perspective on this article?

6. Compare the headlines of "Cocaine Billionaires: The Men Who Hold Colombia Hostage" (on page 137) and "Guns, Drugs and Money: Taking Down the Drug Kingpin Paul Le Roux" (on page 207). Which is a more compelling headline, and why? How could the less compelling headline be changed to better draw the reader's interest?

7. "A Drug Lord Is Buried as a Folk Hero" (on page 163) features a photograph. What does this photograph add to the article?

8. What type of story is "Pablo Escobar's Home Is Demolished in Colombia, Along With a Painful Legacy" (on page 167)? Can you identify another article in this collection that is the same type of story? What elements helped you come to your conclusion?

9. What is the intention of the article "30 Indicted in Queens in Heroin Crackdown" (on page 174)? How effectively does it achieve its intended purpose?

10. Often, as a news story develops, a journalist's attitude toward the subject may change. Compare "In Real Life, 'Rambo' Ends Up as a Soldier of Misfortune, Behind Bars" (on page 191) and "U.S. Reveals Criminal Boss's Role in Capturing a Mercenary" (on page 199), both by Alan Feuer. Did new information discovered between the publication of these two articles change Alan Feuer's perspective?

11. "Guns, Drugs and Money: Taking Down the Drug Kingpin Paul Le Roux" (on page 207) is an example of a critical review. What is the purpose of a critical review? Do you feel this article achieved that purpose?

Citations

All citations in this list are formatted according to the Modern Language Association's (MLA) style guide.

BOOK CITATION

THE NEW YORK TIMES EDITORIAL STAFF. *Drug Kingpins: The People Behind Drug Trafficking.* New York: New York Times Educational Publishing, 2021.

ONLINE ARTICLE CITATIONS

AHMED, AZAM. "El Chapo, Escaped Mexican Drug Lord, Is Recaptured in Gun Battle." *The New York Times*, 8 Jan. 2016, https://www.nytimes.com /2016/01/09/world/americas/El-Chapo-captured-mexico.html.

AHMED, AZAM. "El Chapo, Mexican Drug Kingpin, Is Extradited to U.S." *The New York Times*, 19 Jan. 2017, https://www.nytimes.com/2017/01/19/world /el-chapo-extradited-mexico.html.

AHMED, AZAM. "Mexico, Signaling Shift, Extradites Drug Kingpins to United States." *The New York Times*, 30 Sept. 2015, https://www.nytimes.com/2015 /10/01/world/americas/mexico-signaling-shift-extradites-drug-kingpins -to-united-states.html.

ARCHIBOLD, RANDAL C. "Drug Kingpin Is Captured in Mexico Near Border." *The New York Times*, 15 July 2013, https://www.nytimes.com/2013/07 /16/world/americas/drug-kingpin-is-captured-in-mexico-near-border .html.

ARCHIBOLD, RANDY. "Searching for El Chapo From the Sports Desk." *The New York Times*, 15 July 2015, https://www.nytimes.com/times-insider /2015/07/15/searching-for-el-chapo-from-the-sports-desk/.

BERKE, RICHARD L. "Latin Drug Cartels, Squeezed, Are Turning to Ecuador." *The New York Times*, 25 Mar. 1990, https://timesmachine.nytimes.com /timesmachine/1990/03/25/477790.html.

BROOKE, JAMES. "Cali, the 'Quiet' Drug Cartel, Profits by Accommodation."

The New York Times, 14 July 1991, https://timesmachine.nytimes.com /timesmachine/1991/07/14/939091.html.

BROOKE, JAMES. "Colombia Marvels at Drug Kingpin: A Chain-Saw Killer, Too?" *The New York Times*, 21 June 1995, https://timesmachine.nytimes .com/timesmachine/1995/06/21/069295.html.

BROOKE, JAMES. "A Drug Lord Is Buried as a Folk Hero." *The New York Times*, 4 Dec. 1993, https://timesmachine.nytimes.com/timesmachine/1993/12 /04/665493.html.

BROOKE, JAMES. "Jailed Drug Cartel Chief Still Feared in Colombia." *The New York Times*, 21 Jan. 1992, https://timesmachine.nytimes.com /timesmachine/1992/01/21/276592.html.

BROOKE, JAMES. "Old Drug Allies Terrorizing Escobar." *The New York Times*, 4 Mar. 1993, https://timesmachine.nytimes.com/timesmachine/1993/03 /04/652793.html.

CAVE, DAMIEN. "Arrest of Suspected Drug Lord in Mexico Is Seen as Symbolic Amid Police Scandal." *The New York Times*, 9 Oct. 2014, https://www .nytimes.com/2014/10/10/world/americas/arrest-of-suspected-drug-lord -in-mexico-is-seen-as-symbolic-amid-police-scandal.html.

FEUER, ALAN. "El Chapo Found Guilty on All Counts; Faces Life in Prison." *The New York Times*, 12 Feb. 2019, https://www.nytimes.com/2019/02/12 /nyregion/el-chapo-verdict.html.

FEUER, ALAN. " 'El Chapo' Guzmán Sentenced to Life in Prison, Ending Notorious Criminal Career." *The New York Times*, 17 July 2019, https:// www.nytimes.com/2019/07/17/nyregion/el-chapo-sentencing.html.

FEUER, ALAN. "El Chapo Trial: Why His I.T. Guy Had a Nervous Breakdown." *The New York Times*, 10 Jan. 2019, https://www.nytimes.com/2019/01/10 /nyregion/el-chapo-trial.html.

FEUER, ALAN. "Guns, Drugs and Money: Taking Down the Drug Kingpin Paul Le Roux." *The New York Times*, 5 Mar. 2019, https://www.nytimes.com /2019/03/05/books/review/mastermind-evan-ratliff-paul-le-roux.html.

FEUER, ALAN. "How El Chapo Became a Kingpin, According to a Witness." *The New York Times*, 26 Nov. 2018, https://www.nytimes.com/2018/11/26 /nyregion/el-chapo-witness.html.

FEUER, ALAN. "In El Chapo's Trial, Extraordinary Steps to Keep Witnesses Alive." *The New York Times*, 1 Oct. 2018, https://www.nytimes.com /2018/10/01/nyregion/el-chapo-trial-witnesses.html.

FEUER, ALAN. "In Real Life, 'Rambo' Ends Up as a Soldier of Misfortune,

Behind Bars." *The New York Times*, 20 Dec. 2014, https://www.nytimes
.com/2014/12/21/world/asia/in-real-life-rambo-ends-up-as-a-soldier-of
-misfortune-behind-bars.html.

FEUER, ALAN. "In Spellbinding Testimony, Crime Lord Details Mayhem and Murders." *The New York Times*, 5 Apr. 2018, https://www.nytimes.com/2018/04
/05/nyregion/crime-lord-le-roux-details-mayhem-and-murders.html.

FEUER, ALAN. "Murder Plot Suspect Says Boss Threatened His Life." *The New
York Times*, 13 Jan. 2015, https://www.nytimes.com/2015/01/14/nyregion
/murder-plot-suspect-says-boss-threatened-his-life.html.

FEUER, ALAN. "Prosecutors' Plan for El Chapo: Tie Him to 33 Killings." *The
New York Times*, 30 Oct. 2018, https://www.nytimes.com/2018/10/30
/nyregion/el-chapo-trial-murders.html.

FEUER, ALAN. "The U.S. Case vs. El Chapo: 10,000 Pages and Recordings."
The New York Times, 5 May 2017, https://www.nytimes.com/2017/05/05
/nyregion/el-chapo-size-of-case.html.

FEUER, ALAN. "U.S. Reveals Criminal Boss's Role in Capturing a Mercenary."
The New York Times, 1 Feb. 2015, https://www.nytimes.com/2015/02/02
/nyregion/us-reveals-criminal-bosss-role-in-capturing-a-mercenary.html.

FEUER, ALAN. "Wanted: 12 People Willing to Serve as Jurors in El Chapo
Trial." *The New York Times*, 5 Nov. 2018, https://www.nytimes.com
/2018/11/05/nyregion/el-chapo-trial-jury.html.

FEUER, ALAN, AND EMILY PALMER. "El Chapo's Defense: He Was Framed by
Vast Conspiracy." *The New York Times*, 13 Nov. 2018, https://www.nytimes
.com/2018/11/13/nyregion/el-chapo-trial.html.

FEUER, ALAN, AND EMILY PALMER. "El Chapo's Early Days as a Budding
Kingpin." *The New York Times*, 2 Dec. 2018, https://www.nytimes.com
/2018/12/02/nyregion/el-chapo-trial.html.

GERSTON, JILL. "19 Indicted in Heroin Traffic in City." *The New York Times*,
30 Jan. 1975, https://timesmachine.nytimes.com/timesmachine/1975
/01/30/76335492.html.

GRILLO, IOAN. "El Chapo Puts the Drug War on Trial." *The New York Times*,
15 Nov. 2018, https://www.nytimes.com/2018/11/15/opinion/el-chapo-trial
-drug-war.html.

JONES, RICHARD G. "A New Jersey Crime Story's Hollywood Ending." *The
New York Times*, 1 Nov. 2007, https://www.nytimes.com/2007/11/01
/nyregion/01gangster.html.

KURTZ-PHELAN, DANIEL. "The Long War of Genaro García Luna." *The New*

York Times, 13 July 2008, https://www.nytimes.com/2008/07/13/magazine/13officer-t.html.

MCFADDEN, ROBERT D. "Frank Lucas Dies at 88; Drug Kingpin Depicted in 'American Gangster.'" *The New York Times*, 31 May 2019, https://www.nytimes.com/2019/05/31/obituaries/frank-lucas-dead.html.

MCKINLEY, JAMES C., JR. "In Mexico, a Fugitive's Arrest Captivates the Cameras." *The New York Times*, 12 Oct. 2007, https://www.nytimes.com/2007/10/12/world/americas/12mexico.html.

MCKINLEY, JAMES C., JR. "Mexico Sends 4 Kingpins to Face Trial in the U.S." *The New York Times*, 21 Jan. 2007, https://www.nytimes.com/2007/01/21/world/americas/21mexico.html.

NEUMAN, WILLIAM. "As Drug Kingpins Fall in Mexico, Cartels Fracture and Violence Surges." *The New York Times*, 12 Aug. 2015, https://www.nytimes.com/2015/08/13/world/americas/as-mexico-arrests-kingpins-cartels-splinter-and-violence-spikes.html.

THE NEW YORK TIMES. "Bogotá Drug War Set Back by Court." *The New York Times*, 5 May 1993, https://timesmachine.nytimes.com/timesmachine/1993/05/05/509093.html.

THE NEW YORK TIMES. "Convict Ran Drug Ring." *The New York Times*, 17 Sept. 1977, https://timesmachine.nytimes.com/timesmachine/1977/09/17/76639161.html.

THE NEW YORK TIMES. "Escobar Offers to Yield and Colombia Likes Terms." *The New York Times*, 18 Mar. 1993, https://timesmachine.nytimes.com/timesmachine/1993/03/18/096893.html.

THE NEW YORK TIMES. "Escobar Suggests He May Surrender." *The New York Times*, 9 Sept. 1992, https://timesmachine.nytimes.com/timesmachine/1992/09/09/220792.html.

THE NEW YORK TIMES. "Lawyer Is Indicted on Perjury Counts for '75 Testimony." *The New York Times*, 30 Jan. 1977, https://timesmachine.nytimes.com/timesmachine/1977/01/30/113454587.html.

THE NEW YORK TIMES. "Surrender in Colombia." *The New York Times*, 22 June 1991, https://timesmachine.nytimes.com/timesmachine/1991/06/22/584591.html.

RIDING, ALAN. "Cocaine Billionaires: The Men Who Hold Colombia Hostage." *The New York Times*, 8 Mar. 1987, https://timesmachine.nytimes.com/timesmachine/1987/03/08/938087.html.

RIDING, ALAN. "Colombia Starts to Feel Side Effects of Drug Trade." *The*

New York Times, 20 May 1984, https://timesmachine.nytimes.com
/timesmachine/1984/05/20/203442.html.

ROHTER, LARRY. "A Web of Drugs and Strife in Colombia." *The New York
Times*, 21 Apr. 2000, https://timesmachine.nytimes.com/timesmachine
/2000/04/21/890537.html.

SCHUMACH, MURRAY. "30 Indicted in Queens in Heroin Crackdown." *The
New York Times*, 5 Apr. 1977, https://timesmachine.nytimes.com
/timesmachine/1977/04/05/75061358.html.

SOMAIYA, RAVI. "How Rolling Stone Handled Ramifications of El Chapo
Exclusive." *The New York Times*, 10 Jan. 2016, https://www.nytimes.com
/2016/01/11/business/media/how-rolling-stone-magazine-handled-a-get
-with-ramifications.html.

SPECIA, MEGAN. "Pablo Escobar's Home Is Demolished in Colombia, Along
With a Painful Legacy." *The New York Times*, 22 Feb. 2019, https://www
.nytimes.com/2019/02/22/world/americas/colombia-pablo-escobars
-medellin.html.

THOMPSON, GINGER, AND JAMES C. MCKINLEY JR. "Mexico's Drug Cartels Wage
Fierce Battle for Their Turf." *The New York Times*, 14 Jan. 2005, https://
www.nytimes.com/2005/01/14/world/americas/mexicos-drug-cartels
-wage-fierce-battle-for-their-turf.html.

WEISER, BENJAMIN. "Ex-Soldier Became Contract Killer, Authorities Say."
The New York Times, 27 Sept. 2013, https://www.nytimes.com/2013/09/28
/nyregion/former-army-sergeant-became-contract-killer-authorities-say
.html.

WEISER, BENJAMIN. "Former Army Sniper Pleads Guilty in Murder-for-Hire
Conspiracy." *The New York Times*, 13 Feb. 2015, https://www.nytimes.com
/2015/02/14/nyregion/former-army-sniper-pleads-guilty-in-murder-for
-hire-conspiracy.html.

Index

This book is current up until the time of printing. For the most up-to-date reporting, visit www.nytimes.com.